A Healer of Nations

*A different look at the parables and sayings of
Jesus of Nazareth*

George Lowell Tollefson

PALO FLECHADO PRESS

A Healer of Nations
© 2019 George Lowell Tollefson

ISBN: 978-1-952026-00-3

Library of Congress Control Number: 2019920878

Palo Flechado Press, Santa Fe, NM

OTHER PHILOSOPHICAL WORKS BY GEORGE LOWELL TOLLEFSON

The Immaterial Structure of Human Experience
Unbridled Democracy

Extracts from *Unbridled Democracy*

Spirit as Universal Consciousness
The Thinking Arts
Ethical Considerations
Moral Democracy

Contents

Preliminary Remarks

The following sayings and parables of Jesus are taken from the Gospel of Matthew. They are here brought under a general survey to demonstrate their unity of meaning and purpose. Was the outlook of Jesus gentle or harsh? Was it embracing or exclusionary? In other words, did he truly believe the God he called "Father" is inclined to destroy a proportion of that of which he alone is the author? It is the opinion of this writer that Jesus' message was intended to be gentle and embracing.

The word "gospel" means "glad tidings." Thus the emphasis is positive in tenor. In spite of certain eschatological statements in the text, the general spirit of these teachings is neither condemnatory nor judgmental. It is compassionate, empathetic, and joyful. It exhibits a God who embraces rather than divides.

The King James version of the Bible has been employed here to avoid copyright issues. The use of this older translation is considered acceptable because the discrepancies which exist in it are minor and do not affect the overall meaning of Jesus' message. However, some alterations have been made by the present writer.

Where the text is quoted, a few word substitutions have been indulged in, such as replacing "thee" or "thou" with "you" and removing the "th" endings from verbs. Other word changes here and there, carefully considered so as not to alter the meaning of the text, have been made to render it closer to modern English prose.

Should the reader have doubts concerning any of these alterations, the text can be found in the Gospel of Matthew. It is presented here in the same order as it is there. This includes what in the common English prose of today would be considered some rather odd punctuation. But all specific references to chapter and verse have been omitted. This has been done to improve the flow of the reading. Nevertheless, any verse can be easily located in the original by noting its order of presentation in this work.

The individual scriptural citations are each followed by an interpretation. The interpretations are based on three principles: (1) God is universal spirit. (2) There is but one spirit. And (3) all material things are a direct and full, though limited, expression of spirit. By "full" is meant that there is but one spirit, one universal consciousness. And it is undividedly expressed in each earthly thing, living and inanimate.

Such a distributed presence without division is the possibility of spirit, which is not the case with the material things which emanate from spirit and condition the perception and conceptualizations of the human mind. Of particular interest is the fact that spirit is fully expressed in each human being. It is the consciousness of that person. But, though there is but one consciousness, as there is one spirit, what a human being is conscious of—that is, the content of his or her consciousness—is less than the complete awareness of universal spirit.

In other words, if spirit is universal consciousness, then each individual human consciousness is that universal consciousness in a self-limiting mode of expression. Accordingly, it can be seen that human existence, though generally unbeknownst to the individual person, is deeply embedded in universal spirit. Thus every human being (every man, woman, and child) is in spiritual fact and moral potential a son of God.

It is in this light that the words of Jesus are interpreted. For it is believed by this author, that this is what he meant to convey to his disciples and to all humankind. In consequence of this outlook on the part of the present author, only those utterances are included here which appear to reflect the consistent and complete system of thought which informed the mind of Jesus.

Other seemingly contradictory statements, such as Jesus' response to Peter's acclamation of him as the "Son of the living God" or the more astringent interpretation of his eschatological pronouncements, resulting from a superficial reading, are left to the disputations of scholars and clerics.

In fact, it is easily observed that many of the incidental teachings not central to the general tenor of his thought appear to be quite harsh in tone and do not integrate well into the uniform body of his gentler, more spiritual vision. However, it is not within the scholarly capacity of this writer to decide if some of this material may have been interpolated into Jesus' message by the writer of the Gospel of Matthew or by the writers of the other gospels. In some cases it is simply a matter of interpretation, as in the instance of determining what Peter meant by his proclamation concerning Jesus or how Jesus himself may have understood that proclamation.

Perhaps Jesus was influenced at times by the more astringent teachings of John the Baptist or some others. Whatever is the case, it is evident that there is a nobler and, it should be noted, more otherworldly vision contained in the gentler teachings. For these comprise a thoroughly integrated body of thought making up the principal text of the spoken insights of the man who declared, "My kingdom is not of this world." Thus it is these sayings and parables which are emphasized here.

No emphasis is placed here on the miracles of Jesus or on the healing ministry which he is reported to have carried out. This omission is not an attempt to deny them or some portion of them. It is simply an expedient followed in order to concentrate on the central message. Nor are the passion and the resurrection considered. Again, neither a denial nor an affirmation of these things will be found in this short work. For the spiritual message stands in its integrity with or without them.

It is the opinion of the present author that the system of thought presented here exhibits the most positive and perfect moral and spiritual program ever propounded. However, this does not mean that it is an ethical system in the philosophical sense. Nor is it in any way exclusionary and contradictory of the principal spirit of the teachings of someone like the Buddha. For there is no rational approach to any of these sayings or parables by which they may be fitted into an irrefutable logical structure.

They are much more imaginative and intuitive than such a rigid scheme would allow. In other words, they extend beyond the confines of human perception and reason. Because this is the case, Jesus' teachings cannot be challenged in piecemeal fashion, as could the precepts of a rational ethical system. Nor can the whole tenor of his message be pitted against the insights of another deep spiritual seer.

Only when taken together in a holistic manner are these teachings transformed into a unified spiritual vision which is imaginatively and emotionally apprehended by the mind. Even so, in spite of a lack of rational support, this vision, if properly understood and embraced, could prove to be transformative to the human race. Perhaps this is so *because* it is not a rational system.

Once the spiritual character of human existence is understood in these terms, a new vision and a renewed moral character must fall effortlessly into place. Nevertheless, in perusing these sayings and parables, it should be kept in mind that, in accordance with the fashion of his time, Jesus often used hyperbole to clarify and emphasize his point.

Hence, it it not necessary to assume that by faith one can or should attempt to literally move mountains. Nor is it necessary to assume that a mustard seed will produce a large tree in which birds will make their nests. Rather, it is sufficient to simply imagine these situations in order to arrive at a understanding of the meaning of Jesus' words. Thus, when he spoke of moving mountains, he was clearly not speaking in literal terms. Nor was he doing so in the case of the mustard seed.

Likewise, in a similar manner, when he said that one should pluck out one's eye, give away one's cloak, etc., such observations were expressive of an overall attitude of faith, spiritual determination, and forbearance. Like his fellow human beings, Jesus was a denizen of this material realm. But, unlike most of them, he was profoundly aware of his spiritual origin.

His kingdom was not of this world in the sense that it had no application to a materially minded human race. Such a race, left unaltered, was lost in his opinion. But it could not remain lost. Neither could there be any compromise between spiritual mindedness and material mindedness, such as is exhibited in a religious practice carried out without spiritual insight and personal transformation. Rather, his vision foresaw a return home of humankind as it rediscovers the spiritual origin (lost in early childhood) from which each individual life has become alienated by a sensory-entrapped state of mind.

The Text

Here are the sayings and parables accompanied by a spiritual interpretation. The spiritual interpretation attempts to view them holistically, rather than as individual moral precepts and isolated homilies. Again, chapter and verse are not given. But, for any who wish to seek verification, they are presented in the order in which they are found in the Gospel of Matthew.

Man shall not live by bread alone, but by every word that proceeds out of the mouth of God.

People are spirit and, to be free and fulfilled, must live in the spirit.

You shall not tempt the Lord your God.

Do not act out of the ego. The ego is the material use of spirit, or consciousness, and leads to the wrong results.

You shall worship the Lord your God, and him only shall you serve.

As creatures of spirit, you must be fully spirit in your awareness. To ignore the spirit at the core of your being is to live on the surface of your being. This is a living death.

Repent: for the kingdom of heaven is at hand.

Put away the material mind-set and adopt the mind-set of spirit. Spirit is closer to you than any material thing, including your material awareness of yourself and the world.

Follow me, and I will make you fishers of men.

As you follow my example, so will others follow yours. This is how a life in the spirit is communicated to others: by example.

Blessed are the poor in spirit: for theirs is the kingdom of heaven.

Happy and fulfilled are those of you who have embodied yourselves in spirit. For spirit is what you are.

Blessed are they that mourn: for they shall be comforted.

Spirit will support you in the tribulations of material life. As you live in the spirit, your mind will be enlarged beyond material limitation. As your mind is, so will you be.

Blessed are the meek: for they shall inherit the earth.

Ground your activities not in your material self. For that is the realm of ego. The ego is filled with itself at the expense of others. So ground your activities in the spirit. This will bring a harmony between you and what you experience and do. It requires no thrusting forth of the material self. It is the path of wisdom.

Blessed are they which do hunger and thirst after righteousness: for they shall be filled.

Happy and fulfilled are those who pursue virtue and justice. For, as they are anchored in spirit, so shall they be in accord with themselves and their experience of life. This does not mean everything in material existence will be easy. But, whatever circumstances may arise, they can be met without the anguish of material isolation and loneliness.

Blessed are the merciful: for they shall obtain mercy.

To be merciful is to consider others on a par with yourself. Only the spirit is perfect harmony. So let the spirit guide and encompass your life. Without an awareness of the spirit, all people fall short of this harmony due to the limitations of the material mind. So do not give in to the divisiveness which arises in the material mind and sets one person against another. For that is the limited expression which leads to personal isolation and spiritual death. Whereas a spiritual mind-set encompasses others and invites the same in return.

Blessed are the pure in heart: for they shall see God.

Happy and fulfilled are those whose acts proceed from a spiritual mind. For both they and the universal spirit are one. The spirit is the pure heart which lies deeper in the person and closer to eternal truth than does the material heart of the ego.

Blessed are the peacemakers: for they shall be called the children of God.

Happy and fulfilled are those who live in the unity of spirit. For there is no divisiveness in spirit. Thus there is no conflict.

Blessed are they which are persecuted for righteousness sake: for theirs is the kingdom of heaven.

Happy and fulfilled are those who are persecuted for the sake of virtue, justice, and the life of the spirit. For they are grounded in spirit, where these values prevail. The universal spirit is the kingdom of heaven. Such a grounding offers a greater peace than can be found without it.

Blessed are you when men shall revile you and persecute you and shall say all manner of evil against you falsely for my sake. Rejoice and be exceeding glad: for great is your reward in heaven: for so persecuted they the prophets which were before you.

Happy and fulfilled are you for living in the spirit as I do, even when others do not understand you and condemn you. Rejoice and be very glad. For a life in the spirit brings you peace and a grounding in the eternal, which a life in the material cannot do. In the past, great people of the spirit have done the same.

You are the salt of the earth: but if the salt has lost its savor, wherewith shall it be salted? it is thenceforth good for nothing, but to be cast out, and to be trodden under foot of men.

You exist in the material. But you are more than that. You proceed from spirit. And spirit gives meaning to the material. So, if you have lost your spiritual grounding, where will it be found? Your material existence is then meaningless. In such a condition, you become lost and forgotten, like all material things which are only understood to be material.

You are the light of the world. A city that is set on a hill cannot be hidden. Neither do men light a candle and put it under a bushel, but on a candlestick; and it gives light to all that are in the house. Let your light so shine before men, that they may see your good works and glorify your Father which is in heaven.

You are an example to others. Do not enclose the spirit within yourself. But let it be seen in your attitude and actions. This you cannot help but do, if you live in the spirit. And others will understand that it is so.

Think not that I am come to destroy the law or the prophets: I am not come to destroy, but to fulfill. For truly I say to you, Till heaven and earth pass, one jot or one tittle shall in no wise pass from the law, till all be fulfilled. Whoever therefore shall break one of these least commandments, and shall teach men to do so, he shall be called the least in the kingdom of heaven: but whoever shall do and teach them, the same shall be called great in the kingdom of heaven. For I say to you, That except your righteousness shall exceed the righteousness of the scribes and Pharisees, you shall in no case enter into the kingdom of heaven.

Do not think that I am here to destroy the moral tradition which has been passed down to you. I am here to fulfill it. For I say with certainty that, until the material order is entirely subsumed under the spiritual order, the tradition remains as a guide. So, whoever ignores this wisdom and advises others to do so places himself far from the spirit. But whoever exercises this wisdom and leads others to understand it is well grounded in the spirit. For I tell you, to be spiritual you must act wisely and not merely speak of spiritual matters.

You have heard that it was said by them of old time, You shall not kill; and whoever shall kill shall be in danger of the judgment: But I say to you, that whoever is angry with his brother without a cause shall be in danger of the judgment: and whoever shall say to his brother, Raca, shall be in danger of the council: but whoever shall say, You fool, shall be in danger of hell fire. Therefore if you bring your gift to the altar, and there remember that your brother has ought against you; leave there your gift before the altar, and go your way; first be reconciled to your brother, and then come and offer your gift.

Traditional law condemns the outward act. But it is the inward attitude which reveals the spirit. Human beings are all one in spirit. So any discord between them is an indication of the divisiveness of a material perspective. Furthermore, to judge that another person is morally worthless, empty of inner purpose, or outside of the domain of spirit, when you cannot see that person's heart, is to put yourself in question as well, or even cast yourself outside the domain of spirit altogether. For these reasons, if you are attempting to live in the spirit, and find yourself unjustly at odds with another person, put away your grudge and heal the breach, so that you both may continue in the unity of the spirit.

Agree with your adversary quickly, while you are in the way with him; lest at any time the adversary deliver you to the judge, and the judge deliver you to the officer, and you be cast into prison. Truly I say to you, you shall by no means come out thence, till you have paid the uttermost farthing.

Do not let divisiveness be a cause of further divisiveness, lest you become so deeply embedded in material divisiveness that you have lost your way.

You have heard that it was said by them of old time, You shall not commit adultery: But I say to you, That whoever looks on a woman to lust after her has committed adultery with her already in his heart.

The outward act is an expression of the inward character of mind. So, where the act does not occur, perhaps for fear or for lack of an opportunity, yet the character of mind which could produce the act exists, the inner person is equally compromised. For it is his spiritual state which is most in question, not his material condition.

And if your right eye offends you, pluck it out and cast it from you: for it is profitable for you that one of your members should perish, and not that your whole body should be cast into hell. And if your right hand offends you, cut it off and cast it from you: for it is profitable for you that one of your members should perish, and not that your whole body should be cast into hell.

Nothing in your material person or possession is worth the loss of your life in the spirit.

It has been said, Whoever shall put away his wife, let him give her a writing of divorcement: But I say to you, That whoever shall put away his wife, saving for the cause of fornication, causes her to commit adultery: and whoever shall marry her that is divorced commits adultery.

Though all human beings are ultimately one in spirit, a marriage is yet a committed union between two persons recognizing their spiritual oneness under the condition of their material separateness. It is a bond of trust. And trust is an affirmation of the unity of spirit. So to break the bond of trust is to break the unity of spirit in your mind and to depart from the spirit altogether. For to betray a person in this way causes that person to seek another union, as though such unions were only material and not an entering into the condition of spirit. Moreover, to come into union with one cast off from an existing union is to foster spiritual division. This cannot be, since spirit is indivisible.

Again, you have heard that it has been said by them of old time, You shall not forswear yourself, but shall perform to the Lord your oaths: but I say to you, Swear not at all; neither by heaven; for it is God's throne: Nor by the earth; for it is his footstool: neither by Jerusalem; for it is the city of the great King. Neither shall you swear by your head, because you cannot make one hair white or black. But let your communication be, Yes, yes; No, no: for whatever is more than these comes from evil.

Do not express or undergo any kind of oath. For these limit you by placing your integrity outside of yourself. They are inevitably based on material circumstance and not on the inner spirit, which, in each person's case, is known by that person alone. So stand on who you are in spirit and act out of that. There is no higher authority than spirit.

You have heard that it has been said, An eye for an eye, and a tooth for a tooth: But I say to you, That you resist not evil: but whoever shall smite you on your right cheek, turn to him the other also. And if any man will sue you at the law and take away your coat, let him have your cloak also. And whoever shall compel you to go a mile, go with him two. Give to him who asks you, and from him that would borrow from you turn not away.

It is of the character of a life in the spirit, that material considerations are of less importance than spiritual. To resist evil is to enter into the character of the material. It is the attitude of a divisive world and a divisive mind. And spirit is not divisive. However, this does not imply a complete ignoring of material circumstance or a sacrifice of yourself. Such a sacrifice would offend the integrity of spirit. For you are an expression of God. Would you sacrifice the ground of all being for the sake of some momentary material occurrence, a particular mode of that being? The whole is greater than its individual expressions. Rather, what "resist not evil" means is that all things should be done with forbearance and understanding. Both you and another person stand together in the dignity of spirit. What offends either one of you offends the other. So a carefully considered balance must be achieved. And where such a balance is not clear, it is better to go the extra mile.

You have heard that is has been said, You shall love your neighbor and hate your enemy. But I say to you, Love your enemies, bless them that curse you, do good to them that hate you, and pray for them which despitefully use you and persecute you; That you may be the children of your Father which is in heaven: for he makes his sun to rise on the evil and on the good and sends rain on the just and on the unjust. For if you love them which love you, what reward have you? do not even the publicans the same? And if you salute your brethren only, what do you more than others? do not even the publicans so? Be you therefore perfect, even as your Father which is in heaven is perfect.

Perfection lies in the character of spirit. It is not a matter of degree but of kind. To place one's mind within the realm of spiritual understanding (insofar as that is possible to finite awareness) is to live in the character of spirit. All people are one spirit in God. Yet the limitations of the material make it appear otherwise. For this reason, in order to rise above the limitations of a material mind-set, treat all people with respect and forbearance, as you would treat the farthest extremity of your body. Would you cut off your foot because it tripped you? To injure anyone or wish them ill is to injure yourself.

Take heed that you do not your alms before men, to be seen of them: otherwise you have no reward of your Father which is in heaven. Therefore when you do your alms, do not sound a trumpet before you, as the hypocrites do in the synagogues and in the streets, that they may have glory of men. Truly I say to you, They have their reward. But when you do alms, let not your left hand know what your right hand does: That your alms may be in secret: and your Father which sees in secret himself shall reward you openly. And when you pray, you shalt not be as the hypocrites are: for they love to pray standing in the synagogues and in the corners of the streets, that they may be seen of men. Truly I say to you, They have their reward. But you, when you pray, enter into your closet, and when you have shut your door, pray to your Father which is in secret; and your Father which sees in secret shall reward you openly.

Life comes from the spirit, not from social placement. Invest your sense of self in an inward spiritual purpose. And your proper position in the material realm will follow. To make a show of your goodness or your piety is to have no part in either. These are spiritual properties, coming naturally to those who fully live them. True goodness and piety cannot be divided up and parcelled out. For they arise from within the holistic nature of spirit. Their material fruits, therefore, are just the season's fruits, to be brought forth, dispensed, and regenerated. They are not the life of the tree.

But when you pray, use not vain repetitions, as the heathen do: for they think that they shall be heard for their much speaking. Be not you therefore like them: for your Father knows what things you have need of before you ask him.

Be honest and direct in your praying. A prayer is an address to your innermost being, your consciousness, which is a limited expression of the greater consciousness of God. Your consciousness, when considered without regard to material experience, is spirit. So your prayer is spirit communing with spirit. And, as there is only one spirit, from which all things derive their origin, it is an intimacy in which there are no unshared secrets. For in the timeless domain of universal spirit, all things are immediate and known.

After this manner therefore pray: Our Father which is in heaven, Hallowed be your name. Your kingdom come. Your will be done in earth, as it is in heaven. Give us this day our daily bread. And forgive us our debts, as we forgive our debtors. And lead us not into temptation, but deliver us from evil: For yours is the kingdom, and the power, and the glory, for ever. Amen.

The meaning of this prayer is: All things are in the spirit, which is the source and sustainer of material existence. Human beings should respect the spirit and desire that things be in accord with it. Each person should remember that her and any other person's dependence on the spirit is greater than any person's dependence on any other thing or another person. So human actions should be drawn from and directed toward the spirit, exhibiting tolerance and forbearance in material matters. And a person should always seek the life of the spirit in herself, so as to be led by it and not fall into the divisiveness of the material mind-set. She should willingly promote, not hinder, the life of the spirit in others.

For if you forgive men their trespasses, your heavenly Father will also forgive you: But if you forgive not men their trespasses, neither will your Father forgive your trespasses.

Motives, such as those which lead to an unforgiving attitude, are embedded in material things. They are a product of vanity, which is based on a sense of personal limitation and isolation from others. Coupled with this sense of personal limitation is a vague recognition that a unity of spirit is reflected in the unity of personal consciousness. So vanity arises in a person's mind because that person is cut off from this unity of spirit. Vanity is the person's attempt to compensate for it by seeking to erect a material unity of personal influence over others. When another person insults or harms the interests of this person, there is a sense of diminishment of the injured person. So he retaliates. But, in the end, there is no harmony in such a limited state of mind, no peace, no rest. So, to achieve a true and lasting harmony, it is necessary to draw on the resources of the inward spirit, which lies at the core of every person's awareness, and which is where an origin common to others can be found. Moreover, if such a harmony is sought—and why would it not be, once it is discovered and understood?—it is imperative that any one person should not be a reason that others remain in a spirit of divisiveness and enmity. For divisiveness continues to exist where unity is incomplete.

Moreover when you fast, be not, as the hypocrites, of a sad countenance: for they disfigure their faces, that they may appear to men to fast. Truly I say to you, They have their reward. But you, when you fast, anoint your head, and wash your face; That you appear not to men to fast, but to your Father which is in secret: and your Father, which sees in secret, shall reward you openly.

Fasting is for the purpose of achieving greater spiritual focus. So when you fast, make it sincere, an act of the spirit and not an act of vanity, which latter only serves a material purpose. Those who act out of vanity receive the material rewards of vanity, which are fleeting in character and unsatisfying. The reward of spiritual sincerity is a deep inner grounding in your eternal self.

Lay not up for yourselves treasures upon earth, where moth and rust corrupt and where thieves break through and steal: But lay up for yourselves treasures in heaven, where neither moth nor rust corrupt, and where thieves do not break through nor steal: For where your treasure is, there will your heart be also.

You cannot enhance the inner life with outward things. Yet you are that inner life and not the outer things, which are fickle and soon lost. If you place your interest in the outward things of the material world, you will identify with the false material self and become caught up both physically and mentally in its environment of appearance. And you will perish. But, if you focus your attention on the inner self, which is the imperishable spirit, then you can live in the material world without being consumed by it.

The light of the body is the eye: if therefore your eye be single, your whole body shall be full of light. But if your eye be evil, your whole body shall be full of darkness. If therefore the light that is in you be darkness, how great is that darkness!

Your perspective upon life is important. If it is spiritual, it will guide you in a holistic manner, always cognizant of the final unity of things. This allows all things and events to take on their proper value. In this way, the spiritual perspective becomes a proper guide. But, if your perspective is material, you will live in the midst of and be consumed by the divisiveness and limitation of material things and events. And your awareness of the spirit within you will be extinguished. So, if the life of the spirit within you is extinguished, there is nothing left but a perishable and meaningless outer form. That outer form becomes all that you are.

No man can serve two masters: for either he will hate the one, and love the other; or else he will hold to the one, and despise the other. You cannot serve God and mammon.

No one can be grounded in both the material and the spirit. Your motives come from where you are grounded. You cannot simultaneously live the inner life and derive purpose from material things. The reason for this is that they are contrary to one another. But they do not stand in opposition in the same way. A focus on material things limits the mind until the mind cannot see the holistic unity of spirit. But a focus on the spirit does not limit the mind. For limitation is not the character of spirit, as it is of the material. Spirit is far more inclusive and unifying. And spirit is imperishable. So a focus on spirit places material things in a proper subordinacy.

Therefore I say to you, Take no thought for your life, what you shall eat, or what you shall drink; nor yet for your body, what you shall put on. Is not the life more than meat, and the body than raiment? Behold the fowls of the air: for they sow not, neither do they reap, nor gather into barns; yet your heavenly Father feeds them. Are you not much better than they? Which of you by taking thought can add one cubit to his stature? And why take thought for raiment? Consider the lilies of the field, how they grow; they toil not, neither do they spin: And yet I say to you, That even Solomon in all his glory was not arrayed like one of these. Wherefore, if God so clothes the grass of the field, which today is, and tomorrow is cast into the oven, shall he not much more clothe you, O you of little faith? Therefore take no thought, saying, What shall we eat? or, What shall we drink? or, Wherewithal shall we be clothed? (For after all these things do the Gentiles seek:) for your heavenly Father knows that you have need of all these things. But seek you first the kingdom of God, and his righteousness; and all these things shall be added to you. Take therefore no thought for the morrow: for the morrow shall take thought for the things of itself. Sufficient to the day is the evil thereof.

The life of the spirit encompasses the material. It is the source of the material. Go then to that which is the source of all else and seek the ways of spiritual unity, the uprightness of character which expresses and supports that unity, and a justice toward others which affirms it. In doing this, trust that an answer to material things will be supplied. For a life in the spirit is not a life of the irresponsibility of a fool. Rather, a spiritually informed mind is all the more keenly aware of the true nature of circumstances and enabled to do what is required without fretting or undue preoccupation and concern. Your material requirements may not be met in great measure. There is no need for overabundance. But they will be sufficiently taken care off. For, where there are trials, these must be. That is the nature of material limitation. Yet a way through trials is known to the all-encompassing spirit. So it will be made known to you when the appropriate time arrives. In other words, if you live in a spiritual outlook and faith, you will be sustained in it.

Judge not, that you be not judged. For with what judgment you judge, you shall be judged: and with what measure you mete, it shall be measured to you again. And why behold you the mote that is in your brother's eye, but consider not the beam that is in your own eye? Or how will you say to your brother, Let me pull out the mote out of your eye; and, behold, a beam is in your own eye? You hypocrite, first cast out the beam out of your own eye; and then shall you see clearly to cast out the mote out of your brother's eye.

A judgmental attitude is a critical frame of mind based on the limitations of material things and their comparisons. When people are thus led to turn their attention exclusively to the material, it leads to further judgemental attitudes. For they are apt to clearly see limitation all around them, while overlooking an understanding of their own limitations. But in the spirit, all things are to one unseen purpose, which precludes such comparisons. Furthermore, the fact that material judgments like these are often applied with a different standard toward oneself than to others is what makes them hypocritical. And this leads to anger and reciprocal judgment of like character. So it is good for each person to remember that it is in the nature of material existence to be lacking in many things. All things, including people, come up short of the ideal, except insofar as spirit is applied to by each person as the source of a full and complete understanding of things.

Give not that which is holy unto the dogs, neither cast you your pearls before swine, lest they trample them under their feet, and turn again and rend you.

You cannot confront an unwilling mind with spiritual insight. If another mind is unreceptive to the things of the spirit, it will only see weakness and confusion in you, as it does in the world. So what you have to say will be either refused or mangled in reception. And the interlocutor will come against you for what are seen as your faults.

Ask, and it shall be given you; seek, and you shall find; knock, and it shall be opened to you: For every one that asks receives; and he that seeks finds; and to him that knocks it shall be opened. Or what man is there of you, whom if his son asks for bread, will he give him a stone? Or if he asks for a fish, will he give him a serpent? If you then, being evil, know how to give good gifts to your children, how much more shall your Father which is in heaven give good things to them that ask him?

Ask in the spirit. And the spirit will respond. The spirit will naturally not give what is not good in the spirit. It will give what is good. That is why you should ask "in the spirit." For the values of the spirit are not those of the material. Though this does not mean that material needs will not be taken care of, since they are necessary for the sustaining of life and physical well-being. The spirit is the father because it is the source of all things. Human beings are spirit because they come from spirit. So that which comes from a source is closest to its own true nature, and therefore most content, when it draws from the source.

Therefore all things whatsoever you would that men should do to you, do you even so to them: for this is the law and the prophets.

Treat others as you would be treated. But, in following this rule, it is important to understand that it is a reciprocal command. You are of an equal worth with others. So it is not a command to sacrifice yourself to others, any more than you should expect them to sacrifice themselves to you. As for the law and the prophets, they are principally concerned with the issue of trust.

For example, to create a harmonious social unity, a person must be able to trust others not to steal, injure, or slander her, etc. In other words, they should treat her as they expect her to treat them. Neither should one neglect the unfortunate, as if they were not a part of the human community. Even the command to worship God with all one's heart, mind, and soul is concerned with one's living fully in the spirit in order to form a mind-set which is capable of acting out of spiritual unity and justice.

Enter in at the strait gate: for wide is the gate, and broad is the way, that leads to destruction, and many there be which go in thereat: Because strait is the gate, and narrow is the way, which leads to life, and few there be that find it.

Spiritual life is centered in the purity of human consciousness—the purity of human consciousness being the absence of a reference to the divisiveness of its material content. However, universal consciousness, or spirit, extends well beyond human awareness. So the influence of spirit cannot be seen. It must be felt within one's consciousness. In the rush and pang of material existence, this is easily ignored and therefore difficult to focus on. But it is the only means by which personal fulfilment through unity with the eternal can be achieved.

Beware of false prophets, which come to you in sheep's clothing, but inwardly they are ravening wolves. You shall know them by their fruits. Do men gather grapes of thorns, or figs of thistles? Even so every good tree brings forth good fruit; but a corrupt tree brings forth evil fruit. A good tree cannot bring forth evil fruit, neither can a corrupt tree bring forth good fruit. Every tree that brings not forth good fruit is hewn down, and cast into the fire. Wherefore by their fruits you shall know them.

False prophets are known by their character, and their character by their words and actions. Any presumed expression of spiritual life which is not truly centered in the spirit is another form of the material. Though one can live spiritually in the material, it is not possible to do so while grounding one's motives in the material. What is not of the spirit is quickly perishable and of no account. So a person should beware of anything which has a tincture of vanity in it. Vanity grows out of the pressure to push back against material limitation. It does imply an unacknowledged awareness of spirit. Hence the impulse to resist limitation. But, when the means of resistance are expressions of limitation itself—that is, when they are expressions of vanity— the character of what remains a material mind-set is revealed. Whereas a true acknowledgement of spirit takes on the character of spirit, which is not a futile and divisive resistance. It is at rest, inclusive, and inclined toward intelligent optimism. By "intelligent optimism" is meant an optimism grounded in a clear understanding of circumstances. It is not self-deception or wishful thinking. These again are products of a sense of material limitation and divisiveness.

Not every one that says to me, Lord, Lord, shall enter into the kingdom of heaven; but he that does the will of my Father which is in heaven. Many will say to me in that day, Lord, Lord, have we not prophesied in your name? and in your name have cast out devils? and in your name done many wonderful works? And then will I profess to them, I never knew you:

depart from me, you that work iniquity. Therefore whoever hears these sayings of mine, and does them, I will liken him to a wise man, which built his house upon a rock: And the rain descended, and the floods came, and the winds blew, and beat upon that house; and it fell not: for it was founded upon a rock. And every one that hears these sayings of mine, and does them not, shall be likened to a foolish man, which built his house upon the sand: And the rain descended, and the floods came, and the winds blew, and beat upon that house; and it fell: and great was the fall of it.

Merely professing the ideals of spirit is not enough. Nor is action according to spiritual ideals enough, if it does not proceed directly from the life of the spirit. The spiritual life cannot be approached partially, but must be entered into fully. For it is a transformation of the person out of material consciousness into a complete spiritual awareness. It is an immersion of the person in spiritual consciousness, though, of course, the practical business of material life must continue. Nevertheless, one's motivations must come, not from the divisiveness of material awareness, but from the unity of spirit. This is the rock upon which the house of one's life must be built, if the buffets of material experience are not to blow it over and deliver the person into confusion and the loss of a true and enduring sense of self.

Many shall come from the east and west, and shall sit down with Abraham, and Isaac, and Jacob, in the kingdom of heaven. But the children of the kingdom shall be cast out into outer darkness: there shall be weeping and gnashing of teeth.

Only a full life in the spirit suffices. Material forms, connections, and practices do not matter, if they are not spiritually motivated. The temple religion centered in Jerusalem had grown cold in the lives of many of the common people, particularly those in outlying areas like Galilee. Its forms, rituals, and sacrifices did little to comfort and enlighten the hearts of these people. In other words, temple practices were about God. But they were not spiritual. Not, at any rate, for the individual person. God was a thing apart, out of reach, not an intimacy of connection and a means of self-transformation. It is this transformation which is an entering into the kingdom of heaven. Without it, there is no entering.

And Jesus said to the centurion, Go your way; and as you have believed, so be it done to you.

Where the mind and heart are, that is where the faith is. If the mind and heart are of the spirit, so will be the results. Faith is not just an acceptance of truths which appear to defy material experience. It is a different outlook and attitude. It is a transformation from the prison of material limitation to the freedom of unlimited and eternal spirit. "Eternal" here does not mean "a very long time." For time is a material expression. Eternal spirit is that which simply *is* and sustains every other thing inasmuch as it *is*.

Follow me; and let the dead bury their dead.

Life in the spirit is eternal, not limited by divisiveness and time, which are material. Those who are fully immersed in material-mindedness are the dead. Their concerns are with the dead. But bestowing a greater reverence upon the fleeting appearances of the material is wrong-minded. It neglects that which is not a fleeting appearance: the life of the spirit.

[Concerning the man sick with the palsy, whom Jesus healed and said, "Your sins are forgiven."] For which is easier, to say, Your sins be forgiven you; or to say, Arise, and walk?

To forgive sins is to make a person whole in the spirit. To physically heal them is to make them whole in the body. So which is easier, to make things whole in the spirit or to make them whole in the material? If the material can be made whole, then, clearly, so can the spirit. For it is easier to move the mind than to move those things which lie outside the control of the mind.

Learn what that means, I will have mercy, and not sacrifice.

The spirit of unity in humankind is merciful. For it is inclusive, as spirit is inclusive. The acceptance of sacrifice was an ancient concession made to darkened hearts who did not yet understand the true nature of spirit.

No man puts a piece of new cloth onto an old garment, for that which is put in to fill it up takes from the garment, and the rent is made worse. Neither do men put new wine into old bottles:

29

else the bottles break, and the wine runs out, and the bottles perish: but they put new wine into new bottles, and both are preserved.

The spiritual insights of Jesus transcend the old thinking. They do not destroy the old thinking. But they cast it in a radically new light. So much is this the case, that whatever remains of the old thinking is no longer what it was. It is transformed and made new, so that it may embrace the new. But if the old thinking should remain old, it will conflict with the new. Then the old thinking will be destroyed. And the new will be lost as well. For it will be without a context.

[Concerning the woman, who, seeking healing, touched the hem of Jesus' garment.] Daughter, be of good comfort; your faith has made you whole.

Entering into the unity of spirit, trusting and resting there, can transform the material expression of the person who does this. The woman's mind was whole. As it was such, her body was put into accord with it. It was healed to agree in character with a holistic mind.

The harvest truly is plenteous, but the laborers are few; Pray you therefore the Lord of the harvest, that he will send forth laborers into his harvest.

There are many who long for spiritual comfort. But they do not know how to find it. Yet they are ready to receive spiritual understanding if there are others who will show them the way. So pray that spiritual understanding will be brought forth in the minds of those others, who in turn will bring it forth in many more people.

Freely you have received, freely give.

The spirit and its work are the universal possessions of all. All are an expression of spirit. So to open another person's understanding to spirit is to join them in a common ground which can be achieved in no other or better way. Jesus sought to bring his disciples to a condition like that of himself. He sent them out to do what he had done. But they did not understand him.

The workman is worthy of his meat.

Material needs will follow upon spiritual life. Where one works for a higher purpose, the means of sustenance are often obtained in unexpected ways. This cannot be explained by a material understanding. But it is a common experience of many who have ventured in this direction.

And if the house be worthy, let your peace come upon it: but if it be not worthy, let your peace return to you. And whoever shall not receive you, nor hear your words, when you depart out of that house or city, shake off the dust of your feet. Truly I say to you, It shall be more tolerable for the land of Sodom and Gomorrha in the day of judgment, than for that city.

Spiritual truth is a source of peace. But it can only be received by a mind open to the unity of spirit. It cannot be inserted into a closed material mind. For divisiveness cannot understand unity. Depart from that person (or persons) without resentment. A stubbornly divided mind brings its own judgment upon it. For it remains grounded in personal limitation. And this is a living hell. It is a judgment which is immediate and all-encompassing and therefore timeless.

Behold, I send you forth as sheep in the midst of wolves: be you therefore wise as serpents, and harmless as doves.

The world is governed by divisiveness. And the ways of divisiveness are harmful. So be subtle and perceptive in discernment, but without resentment.

And you shall be brought before governors and kings for my sake, for a testimony against them and the Gentiles.

Some of the people who oppose you will be in high places. They will be foreign to you and will not share your outlook. Nevertheless, by this encounter you will bring the spiritual witness I have shown you before them, though they do not wish to understand it. Yet, having been brought into contact with your character, some of them will be made to question themselves. Others will hear of the encounter and will think about it.

t when they deliver you up, take no thought how or what you shall speak: for it shall be given you in that same hour what you shall speak. For it is not you that speaks, but the Spirit of your Father which speaks in you.

Being of a spiritual mind, what you speak will be from the undivided perspective of eternal spirit, not from the divided mind of perishable physical being. It will come to you naturally, rather

32

than from much thinking. For an unenlightened reason is material and divisive in character. Conversely, when your mind is open and willing, the spiritual state of it will cause you to form insights you would not otherwise have achieved. And words will arise naturally from your own mind to express the insights.

The disciple is not above his master, nor the servant above his lord. It is enough for the disciple that he be as his master, and the servant as his lord.

Nothing is greater than universal spirit. All people are expressions of that spirit in its self-limiting form. Moreover, universal spirit is one spirit which is wholly (but differently) expressed in each of its self-limiting forms. So all people, though individual, are ultimately one in the spirit. In other words, while being materially differentiated, and therefore limited in their material awareness, they are complete expressions of one and the same universal spirit. Each person *is* that one spirit. For this reason, it is enough to express the spirit in one's person. And there can be no motivation to seek an elevation of status over others.

There is nothing covered, that shall not be revealed; and hid, that shall not be known.

Universal spirit, or universal consciousness, is timeless. And all things are within it. For they emanate from it. Moreover, in spirit, where individual spiritual being can yet be expressed, there is a community of awareness of those beings, though not without individuality. In spirit, knowledge moves freely between individual minds. So, since it is human destiny for humankind to

33

rise to a spiritual state of awareness (this destiny determined by the drawing up of human awareness into the liberating condition of pure consciousness), what is to be known to humankind cannot be kept from it forever.

What I tell you in darkness, that speak you in light: and what you hear in the ear, that preach you upon the housetops.

Openly reveal what you have been personally shown.

And fear not them which kill the body, but are not able to kill the soul: but rather fear him which is able to destroy both soul and body in hell.

Do not fear for your physical safety. It is the spirit which endures, not the body. The body and its material experience are together a fleeting appearance, however intensely real and present they may seem in daily life. But human consciousness, which is the spirit, is not a ghost of the material mind, though its fundamental reality is hidden by the felt urgency of material experience. So fear only the divisiveness of mind that arises from this false sense of limitation, which material awareness is able to create when the mind is devoid of spiritual understanding. That false sense of limitation, reflecting a confined awareness, is what leads to the oppression of one person by another and to a general sense of helplessness in the face of the apparent dissolution of all things. It is this kind of fear which destroys the mind of a person. And what greater hell is there than the destruction of one's mind? Nevertheless, the knowledge that all things are grounded in spirit does make it clear that God is directly involved in the mind's limitations. But for any person to remain in a condition of such limitation, without any knowledge of spirit, is not the preferred way of spirit.

Are not two sparrows sold for a farthing? and one of them shall not fall on the ground without your Father. But the very hairs of your head are all numbered. Fear not therefore, you are of more value than many sparrows.

All things are expressions of spirit, which is eternal, or ineradicable. So all things are known to spirit, down to the most minute detail. Their deepest character, their reality, is in spirit. Thus, in an abiding sense, they are ineradicable. But, in addition to this, each person is a conscious being who is able to recognize spirit as the ground of his existence and awareness. So this awareness, especially when centered upon such a spiritual recognition, is ineradicable in a special way which supersedes other things. For it is the eternal consciousness of spirit in its self-limiting mode.

Whoever therefore shall confess me before men, him will I confess also before my Father which is in heaven. But whoever shall deny me before men, him will I also deny before my Father which is in heaven.

Jesus, speaking in a spiritually-minded way, says: I live wholly in the spirit. If you do the same and show this to others, you are in the spirit. And you show others the spirit. If they then deny what you represent, and what I represent, and do not live in the spirit, they deny the spirit. This denial of spirit is the same in result as the spirit denying them. For, by their decision, spiritual life is withdrawn from them.

Think not that I am come to send peace on earth: I came not to send peace, but a sword. For I am come to set a man at variance against his father, and the daughter against her mother, and the daughter in law against her mother in law. And a man's foes shall be they of his own household.

Knowledge of the spirit is like a sword. It cuts to the heart of any human consciousness. But that consciousness may refuse to understand the spirit and will, in such a case, not accept it. So there can be no accord between the unity of spiritual-mindedness and the divisiveness of material-mindedness. For those who are not of the spirit will not understand those who *are* of the spirit and will oppose them. Thus they will be in opposition. This will occur even in the most intimate relationships.

He that loves father or mother more than me is not worthy of me: and he that loves son or daughter more than me is not worthy of me. And he that takes not his cross, and follows after me, is not worthy of me.

Life in the spirit is uncompromising and must come first. Every other thing follows from a life in the spirit. This arises from the simple fact that spirit is more fundamental than its material expressions. To put any aspect of the material before the spirit would be like eating the skin of an apple and throwing away the flesh of it.

He that finds his life shall lose it: and he that loses his life for my sake shall find it.

Human beings find themselves in material circumstances. These are initially embraced. But there is no peace in them. So something better must be found. That something is the life of spirit. To enter into this life, a person must put material circumstances aside. It is to accept and emulate the example of Jesus, which is to turn away from the importance of the material. So the life lost is that of a mind imprisoned in material limitation. The life found is that of spiritual freedom. This freedom lies at the core of human nature, always available, but often unrecognized.

He that receives you receives me, and he that receives me receives him that sent me.

Jesus says: He who follows your spiritual example follows mine. And he who follows my spiritual example enters into the spirit.

He that receives a prophet in the name of a prophet shall receive a prophet's reward; and he that receives a righteous man in the name of a righteous man shall receive a righteous man's reward.

He who recognizes the character of a spiritual person and accepts what that person represents takes part in what he represents and achieves the benefits of a spiritual life.

And whoever shall give to drink to one of these little ones a cup of cold water only in the name of a disciple, verily I say unto you, he shall in no wise lose his reward.

If a person can accept within herself the simplicity and open heart of a small child, she can enter easily into the life of spirit. For a child is closer to its spiritual origin and not bound by the rational constructs of an adult material mind. It is also the case that an act of compassion toward one who is simple of heart indicates a like attitude. Thus even a sympathizer who has not yet achieved full spiritual awareness is in a state of transformation from limitation of mind into spiritual freedom.

And blessed is he, whoever shall not be offended in me.

If what Jesus represents does not upset a person, if it does not represent a threat to his material interests, then he will have understood the life of the spirit and will enter into it happy and fulfilled.

Wisdom is justified of her children.

Those who live in the wisdom of spirit reflect it in their manner. Furthermore, their manner, when widely adopted, can transform the world. It can bring harmony, peace, and a greater and more positive creativity among human beings.

I thank you, O Father, Lord of heaven and earth, because you have hid these things from the wise and prudent, and have revealed them unto babes.

The things of the spirit are those of unity. They cannot be understood by materially divisive minds, so long as those minds use the elements of divisiveness to make their judgments. This results from the fact that a materially inclined intellect employs a limited form of perception to develop its concepts. For this reason, the wisdom of the spirit cannot be found in reasoning alone. So spiritual insights must first be apprehended by minds caught up in the unified perspective of spirit. Only subsequently may these insights be submitted to intellect to be processed in a manner accessible to human understanding. That is why children are cited here. A young child, being less hardened in its thinking by material experience, is more open to the inner workings of spirit.

All things are delivered to me of my Father: and no man knows the Son, but the Father; neither knows any man the Father, save the Son, and he to whomever the Son will reveal him.

Jesus lives completely in the spirit. His mind has become entirely that of the spirit. So he is a fully realized "Son." It is in this way that he is known to the Father. Yet his mind is still individual. And he is physically human. Consequently, he knows only those things of the spirit which pertain to this world. He does not know more than this, as he concedes elsewhere, such as when he tells James and John that they will share in his earthly sacrifices and spiritual anointing but that it is not for him to give them priority in the spirit (quoted later in this work). Even when he shows what would appear to be a transcending knowledge, such as when he states that there is no marriage in the spiritual realm, such knowledge is deduced from the nature of spirit as it is revealed to human experience. For marriage is based on procreation and the need to assuage emotional isolation, neither of which limit-induced conditions reflect the undivided, unifying character of spirit. Now to truly know Jesus is to know the spirit as it is fully manifested in human form. For he has become an expression of it. Thus to know him is to know the spirit. But, if the spirit is not received in the mind and heart of a person, neither is Jesus known to that person.

Come to me, all you that labor and are heavy laden, and I will give you rest. Take my yoke upon you, and learn of me; for I am meek and lowly in heart: and you shall find rest unto your souls. For my yoke is easy, and my burden is light.

All you who are burdened with the tribulations of physical life, find rest in the spirit I represent. Take this life of the spirit upon you and grow in it. That is, learn how it reinterprets and eases the difficulties of life. I am of an open mind, without pretension and material ambition. In such a condition as this you can find rest and an easy refuge. For what I represent is easily entered into. And, once entered into, it settles the mind and heart. It is in this way that peace is found.

Have you not read what David did, when he was hungered, and they that were with him; How he entered into the house of God, and did eat the shewbread, which was not lawful for him to eat, neither for them which were with him, but only for the priests? Or have you not read in the law, how that on the sabbath days the priests in the temple profane the sabbath, and are blameless? But I say to you, That in this place is one greater than the temple. But if you had known what this means, I will have mercy, and not sacrifice, you would not have condemned the guiltless. For the Son of man is Lord even of the sabbath day.

Moral law is made for people. It exists for their good. For this reason, there are exceptions to it, both for expedience and in certain matters of convenience. Moreover, the spirit is present in people and in all things. And the spirit would prefer an attitude of mutual harmony and individual equanimity of character, as opposed to one of isolation and unnecessary personal restraint. In other words, it inclines a person towards a wholesome inclusiveness of others in attitude, rather than toward a further narrowing of attitude through individual acts and collective rites of sacrifice. For sacrifices are made in a divisive spirit, even when they are intended to appease a higher principle or to celebrate a greater unity. The spirit in a human being is greater than any law made for human beings. For moral laws are made so that people may live in harmony with each other, and so that each person may be free of strife, better enabling her to grow in the spirit. Since Jesus was a man entirely immersed in the spirit, he represents living in the spirit. Life in the spirit is the goal of moral law. This makes him greater than the law. Any person fully immersed in and guided by the spirit, as he was, is also greater than the law.

What man shall there be among you, that shall have one sheep, and if it fall into a pit on the sabbath day, will he not lay hold on it, and lift it out? How much then is a man better than a sheep? Wherefore it is lawful to do well on the sabbath days.

What person will not fulfill his responsibility to take care of what is his, even if this responsibility should conflict with the command to rest on the Sabbath day? Would he be at rest if he left this worry unattended? He will attend to it so that he may be at peace, which is the meaning of the Sabbath. To look after another person who is in need is an even greater obligation.

Every kingdom divided against itself is brought to desolation; and every city or house divided against itself shall not stand: And if Satan cast out Satan, he is divided against himself; how shall then his kingdom stand? And if I by Beelzebub cast out devils, by whom do your children cast them out? therefore they shall be your judges. But if I cast out devils by the Spirit of God, then the kingdom of God is come to you. Or else how can one enter into a strong man's house, and spoil his goods, except he first bind the strong man? and then he will spoil his house. He that is not with me is against me; and he that gathers not with me scatters abroad.

Good cannot be accomplished by evil. If a person accomplishes this good, then she does it by the agency of the spirit. How else could it be done, except that something greater, more inclusive, and less divisive than the evil overpowers it? If you are not involved in the life of the spirit, then you are opposed to it. There is no middle ground. For there is no middle ground in spirit. It is not something to be inserted into the midst of a materially oriented life. It is to be exchanged for it. So that a person may live in the material, but not be of it. This is a subtle distinction seen only by the person involved and by those of a similar disposition. But it is a transition in character which will affect the whole of humanity in time. For more will come to see that it is the only way toward harmony and peace. The history of human civilization is less than ten thousand years old. So by the standards of time it is as of now but a very short period.

Wherefore I say to you, All manner of sin and blasphemy shall be forgiven to men: but the blasphemy against the Holy Ghost shall not be forgiven to men. And whoever speaks a word against the Son of man, it shall be forgiven him: but whoever speaks against the Holy Ghost, it shall not be forgiven him, neither in this world, neither in the world to come. Either make the tree good, and his fruit good; or else make the tree corrupt, and his fruit corrupt: for the tree is known by his fruit.

You can momentarily indulge in material-mindedness and yet return to spirit-mindedness. But you cannot reject the spirit altogether. If you do this, what is there that can lead you back to spirit-mindedness? You are lost in the limitations of the material. If you speak against the bearer of the message concerning spirit, the spirit is still open to you. But if you turn against the spirit itself, you will lose it and cannot regain it, either in this life or in the life to come. So either pursue the spirit and accept the gifts of the spirit, or reject it and live in the darkness and limitation of material-mindedness. It is entirely either a matter of the one or the other. For spirit is not division. And division is not spirit. What choice you make will be evident in your attitudes and behavior. (A note on "the world to come": all human beings will be brought into the spiritual fold in time. So, though a person becomes lost in material-mindedness, there is a salvation that is beyond his understanding and present reach. This is so because spirit is undivided and fully encompassing. The fact that the above statement appears to indicate otherwise is due to a *this-world* point of view: in the mind of the spirit-rejecting person, his decision is irremediable.)

O generation of vipers, how can you, being evil, speak good things? for out of the abundance of the heart the mouth speaks. A good man out of the good treasure of the heart brings forth good things: and an evil man out of the evil treasure brings forth evil things. But I say to you, That every idle word that men shall speak, they shall give account of in the day of judgment. For by your words you shall be justified, and by your words you shall be condemned.

The human mind in its accustomed condition is so caught up in the material way of seeing things and the enmity and spite this brings on, it can neither think, act, nor express good things. For out of the mind comes human thought and action. However, if a person is good, then from a good person comes a good state of mind which brings forth a good attitude and good behavior. But a person divided against himself and all others brings forth suspicion, competition, and malice. Therefore, you should understand that everything you do informs not only your present character, but your eternal character. For, as spirit is timeless, so is human character timeless. Both ultimately originate in and are grounded in spirit. Whether this is seen or not seen by the individual person, they are the same. It is this which expresses the finality in personal choice, since that choice brings a person's own judgment upon him. He is in his fundamental nature spirit, however isolated his mind may become from the things of spirit. So his decision is a decision of the spirit, even when it is a wrong decision. Thus the judgment is immediate. And, if it is contrary to spirit, he is out of joint with himself.

When the unclean spirit is gone out of a man, he walks through dry places, seeking rest, and finds none. Then he says, I will return into my house from whence I came out; and when he is come, he finds it empty, swept, and garnished. Then goes he, and takes with himself seven other spirits more wicked than himself, and they enter in and dwell there: and the last state of that man is worse than the first. Even so shall it be also to this wicked generation.

When a negative state of mind has gone out of a person, and the person has not entirely replaced it with a spiritual view, the negative state can return. In other words, if a place remains in the mind where there is doubt and an inclination to cling to material relations, the negative state of mind will return. Since the return of the negative state exhibits a falling back upon the material point of view, the disinclination toward the spirit increases, allowing more and worse negative states to fill the mind. These strengthen the material view. So the person is worse off than before, being more thoroughly ensnared in her limited and strife-torn perspective. This is how it is for the many darkened minds of the present world, even when a number of them have been briefly exposed to a spiritual understanding. For permanently enlightened minds are yet few.

Who is my mother? and who are my brothers? And he stretched forth his hand toward his disciples, and said, Behold my mother and my brothers! For whoever shall do the will of my Father which is in heaven, the same is my brother, and sister, and mother.

The spiritual realm, even on earth, is a community. It is a close community because it is bound together by the unity of spirit. Those who are not of this community remain in a state of mind which in varying degrees isolates them and pits them against one another. So even close physical and emotional relationships in the material world are divided by strife. It is only in the spirit that the strife is taken away and a previously unimaginable closeness is formed. This is why spiritual ties take precedence over earthly connections.

Behold, a sower went forth to sow; And when he sowed, some seeds fell by the way side, and the fowls came and devoured them up: Some fell upon stony places, where they had not much earth: and forthwith they sprung up, because they had no deepness of earth: And when the sun was up, they were scorched; and because they had no root, they withered away. And some fell among thorns; and the thorns sprung up, and choked them: But other fell into good ground, and brought forth fruit, some an hundredfold, some sixtyfold, some thirtyfold. Who has ears to hear, let him hear.

When the message concerning the spirit is presented, it is ignored by some people. Thus it is as if it had not been heard and never delivered in the first place. But other people do hear it and receive it, though it conflicts mightily with the material state of their minds, which is deeply entrenched. So, confronted with the many contrary elements of this state of mind and being opposed by people whose attitudes matter to the person concerned, it cannot develop into a spiritual state of mind. And it is soon abandoned. Yet other people receive the message and make an earnest effort to apply it to themselves. But once again their material inclinations overpower their exertions, which lack sufficient conviction to sustain them in a spiritual state of mind. For these material inclinations are many and in the end more vigorous than the spiritual effort. Finally, there are some people who receive the message fully with an open mind, a willing attitude, and a strong determination to bring themselves in line with it. It is in this case that the spiritual outlook is enabled to change their state of mind. And the newly embraced condition of spiritual-mindedness brings forth attitudes, acts, and personal expressions which are in accordance with the specific character of each person. That is how it is. So, if a person is sufficiently open to this message, let him accept it.

And the disciples came, and said to him, Why do you speak to them in parables? He answered and said to them, Because it is given to you to know the mysteries of the kingdom of heaven, but to them it is not given. For whoever has, to him shall be given, and he shall have more abundance: but whoever has not, from him shall be taken away even that he has. Therefore speak I to them in parables: because they seeing see not; and hearing they hear not, neither do they understand. And in them is fulfilled the prophecy of Esaias, which says, By hearing you shall hear, and shall not understand; and seeing you shall see, and shall not perceive: For this people's heart is waxed gross, and their ears are dull of hearing, and their eyes they have closed; lest at any time they should see with their eyes, and hear with their ears, and should understand with their heart, and should be converted, and I should heal them. But blessed are your eyes, for they see: and your ears, for they hear. For verily I say to you, That many prophets and righteous men have desired to see those things which you see, and have not seen them; and to hear those things which you hear, and have not heard them.

The spirit is within every person. It represents a deeper, more fulfilling life, if it is allowed to develop. But it cannot be ignored. This is because it is not inert. It is life. So it must either grow or diminish within a person. Those who embrace it, develop in it and become spiritually more enriched. But those who reject it lose even what unperceived presence it has had in their lives. For then it is like a candle put out. They live in increasing darkness, as they descend further into strife and the divided state of mind which produces that strife. Since the disciples were following Jesus, the spirit was very much alive in them. It was developing their minds and hearts as they looked to increase its presence in their lives. But many others were too much preoccupied with material concerns and the egoism that accompanies those concerns to be able or willing to receive the message and understand the example of Jesus. Knowing this, he deliberately spoke in such a manner as to make a clear delineation between the willing and the unwilling. Had he not made this distinction, those who were unwilling to accept his message would have found ways to use what they could grasp of it as weapons of endless dispute against his teaching. This would have left him little opportunity to instruct those who were willing, even anxious, to receive his message. But, because the disciples *were* given the opportunity to learn the message, they were enabled to live spiritually enriched lives. Many spokesmen and women of spiritual insight and other good people who had lived prior to Jesus' teaching ministry had longed for this profounder understanding of spiritual life, which they did not fully achieve in their lifetimes.

Hear you therefore the parable of the sower. When any one hears the word of the kingdom, and understands it not, then comes the wicked one, and catches away that which was sown in his heart. This is he which receives seed by the way side. But he that received the seed into stony places, the same is he that hears the word, and anon with joy receives it; Yet has he not root in himself, but lasts for a while: for when tribulation or persecution arises because of the word, by and by he is offended. He also that receives seed among the thorns is he that hears the word; and the care of this world, and the deceitfulness of riches, choke the word, and he becomes unfruitful. But he that receives seed into the good ground is he that hears the word, and understands it; which also bears fruit, and brings forth, some a hundredfold, some sixty, some thirty.

A specifically spiritual explanation of this is given above with the original presentation of the parable.

The kingdom of heaven is likened to a man which sowed good seed in his field: But while men slept, his enemy came and sowed tares among the wheat, and went his way. But when the blade was sprung up, and brought forth fruit, then appeared the tares also. So the servants of the householder came and said to him, Sir, did not you sow good seed in your field? from whence then has it tares? He said to them, An enemy has done this. The servants said to him, Will you then that we go and gather them up? But he said, No; lest while you gather up the tares, you root up also the wheat with them. Let both grow together until the harvest: and in the time of harvest I will say to the reapers, Gather you together first the tares, and bind them in bundles to burn them: but gather the wheat into my barn.

The kingdom of heaven is within a person. It is spirit, or universal consciousness, the true ground of all things. In it there is no final limitation or death. That is to say, in the spiritual realm there may still be a limit of mind conducive to the distinction of personhood. But there will not be the isolating limitations of the material world. But for now, in the material realm, the limitations of material experience have confused people's minds. They have entrapped them in a sense of absolute and spirit-crippling limitation. This causes them to see their individual consciousness as a flickering candle flame, soon to go out. They do not see that it is grounded in an eternal, universal consciousness. For there is only one consciousness. Only the content of human consciousness differs from person to person. But this difference, this limitation of the content of consciousness, can be blinding in its effect. And as the experience of a person's life continues in this crippling vein, he comes to view himself and his world exclusively in terms of the limitations of the material, rather than in terms of the boundless unity and indivisibility of the universal spirit of which his individual existence is an expression. So both spiritual and material perspectives are mixed together within that person, the material exhibiting an increasing dominance. But a time will come among people in general, even in this life, when the spiritual outlook will be fully realized. In that moment (or period of final transformation), the influence of the material perspective as a false sense of limitation will be cleansed from their minds. Yet this cleansing, this removal of the tares in favor of the wholesome fruits of their mind, does not mean that they cannot live in a material world. It simply means that their spirits will not be imprisoned by it.

The kingdom of heaven is like a grain of mustard seed, which a man took, and sowed in his field: Which indeed is the least of all seeds: but when it is grown, it is the greatest among herbs, and becomes a tree, so that the birds of the air come and lodge in the branches thereof.

Every person proceeds from spirit and is spirit in a more fundamental way than she is matter. But in a life of material perceptions, the life of the spirit is obscured. Yet it is there. And, if nurtured, it will grow until a full spiritual life is realized in the person and all things in her life henceforth proceed from spirit. (It is worthy of note at this point to observe how it is that Jesus uses hyperbole, or exaggerated imagery, to emphasize a point. As pointed out in the remarks at the beginning of this work, the mustard seed becoming a tree and providing a means for birds to roost or build their nests is a way of rendering visually acute the abstract principle of the development of full spiritual consciousness in a person.)

The kingdom of heaven is like leaven, which a woman took, and hid in three measures of meal, till the whole was leavened.

This is similar to the quote above it. But what is added is a sense of the internality of spiritual transformation. There is a sense of an expansion of spiritual understanding from a small part of a person's awareness to the whole of it, raising the understanding to a higher level.

Then Jesus sent the multitude away, and went into the house: and his disciples came to him, saying, Declare to us the parable of the tares of the field. He answered and said to them, He that sows the good seed is the Son of man; The field is the world; the good seed are the children of the kingdom; but the tares are the children of the wicked one; The enemy that sowed them is the devil; the harvest is the end of the world; and the reapers are the angels. As therefore the tares are gathered and burned in the fire; so shall it be in the end of this world. The Son of man shall send forth his angels, and they shall gather out of his kingdom all things that offend, and them which do iniquity; And shall cast them into a furnace of fire: there shall be wailing and gnashing of teeth. Then shall the righteous shine forth as the sun in the kingdom of their Father. Who hath ears to hear, let him hear.

Look at the matter not as between individuals, but as within each person. A "Son of man" is a person with the spirit of God *fully expressed* in him or her. That person is a son of God, even when he does not know it. But, when the spirit is expressed in him, though he is yet a human being, he is imbued with the spirit. Thus he is a son of man, or a son of God *in* man. This is what

Jesus was then and what he was teaching his disciples that people in general were destined to be. They are sons of God in regard to their origin in spirit. For their conscious being is an expression of universal consciousness, or spirit. Moreover, they are further destined to become spiritually realized in character. When transformed in this way, they are considered to be sons of men. For the divisive behaviors arising from material states of mind are removed from them. It is through the example and teachings of such a son (and later more sons) that the maturation of spirit within people will be accomplished. At first, people will have both the material outlook and the spiritual view within them. But in time the spiritual will prevail. However, this cannot be brought about without some anguish, as anyone who has undergone a significant change of outlook knows. Generally, it is the case that a person comes to recognize his need for a change in outlook by just such anguish arising from within his materially imprisoned mind. He looks for a way to free himself and finds it in the spirit. In the end, spiritual life will attain its rightful place in the hearts and minds of all people. Most of this will occur in a late transformation. But it will have been prefigured by an intrepid few. In this way, those who are presently willing to make the transition are the ones who are taking the first steps.

Again, the kingdom of heaven is like treasure hidden in a field; the which when a man has found, he hides, and for joy thereof goes and sells all that he has, and buys that field. Again, the kingdom of heaven is like a merchant man, seeking goodly pearls: Who, when he had found one pearl of great price, went and sold all that he had, and bought it.

Once the liberating experience of the spirit is understood and embraced, it is the most important thing in a person's life. Everything else is placed in a state of lesser regard. But this does not mean that everything else is placed in a state of no regard. The same spirit which brings freedom and peace to the mind and heart is the spirit which fills the mind with its perceptions of the world. In this life people are meant to live in the world. But they should have an appropriate concern for inner and outer things, which places the inner life at the head of the outer.

Again, the kingdom of heaven is like a net, that was cast into the sea, and gathered of every kind: Which, when it was full, they drew to shore, and sat down, and gathered the good into vessels, but cast the bad away. So shall it be at the end of the world: the angels shall come forth, and sever the wicked from among the just, And shall cast them into the furnace of fire: there shall be wailing and gnashing of teeth.

The spirit will triumph over humanity at large, as well as over individuals. But it cannot do this without anguish. For a pulling away from the material mind-set is fraught with all the contradictions and oppositions of will that a divisive material world can induce. The transition from material to spiritual life is like a childbirth in which the pains of delivery are soon to be forgotten in a joy for the living child. This may be true of physical suffering and death too, though it is a hard thing to accept the idea that the pain and suffering of this life would seem to be so little in comparison to a later joy. Nevertheless, whatever might be an explanation of present misfortune, the good things of the spirit will come. And they will be aided in their coming forth by those already of a spiritual mind-set. For such people lead the way as an example. Nevertheless, it is important to recognize that, though such examples may assist the transformation, they are not the final cause of its being realized. Rather, universal spirit draws humanity to itself because it lies at the core of human nature and experience, where it exemplifies restful unity in a wholesomeness and purity of being. Every person knows there is something eternal in them, something unlimited and indivisible. It is their consciousness, when that consciousness is considered without regard to its content. This is their inner self, the ground of their awareness. So, to begin their transformation, it is only a matter of acknowledging that this is so. When the individual and, in time, the whole of humankind has been turned about in this way, any dominance over the mind of the limiting thoughts of the material will have been removed and discarded.

Jesus said to them, Have you understood all these things? They said to him, Yes, Lord. Then said he to them, Therefore every scribe which is instructed unto the kingdom of heaven is like a man that is a householder, which brings forth out of his treasure things new and old.

Jesus' grasp of the scriptural tradition differs from those who came before him. He teaches a deeper understanding of the wisdom of the past. And he adds new insights which had not been seen before him. There is also the general fact, applying to him as well as to any other teacher of spiritual truths, that growth in the spirit involves a better understanding of experience and a development of new insights concerning it. So, once a spiritual understanding of experience is achieved, then a person will see past and present things together in a new light and will not only discover, but bring out, the good in them.

Jesus said to them, A prophet is not without honor, save in his own country, and in his own house.

People often refuse to believe that new and startling truths can come from a familiar source. The reason for this is that they have not previously encountered them in the person who is expressing them. And now they are expected to receive the strange and unfamiliar. Moreover, they are expected to accept it from what they recognize as a commonplace source. This means not only encountering a new way of seeing things, but also being confronted by something suddenly and unpleasantly elevating about the messenger. It is a double disturbance of a person's preconceptions which is too much for her.

O you of little faith, wherefore did you doubt?

The spiritual transformation of a life can only occur where a material attitude has been completely put aside. When Peter attempted to walk on water, he still understood the world in a material manner. For that reason, once his mind went to work, he could no longer do it. (Note: The writer of the present book is not a person who professes miracles which overturn natural law. But neither is he a denier of miracles as such. It is his assumption that what are experienced as miracles are genuine but generally unobtrusive and personal. For this reason, they are usually accommodated by subjective modifications in the individual's mind, which incorporate the anomaly into a continuing rational view. This occurs even where more than one person may be involved in the experience. Each person makes her mental accommodation in a similar way. And these people may agree between them that something extraordinary has taken place. Yet the world in general retains its customary relations: it follows natural laws. If miracles are regarded in this light, it may seem as if many of the highly dramatic ones encountered in scripture, like the one about Jesus and Peter walking on water, are exaggerated. Thus it could be that they have been embellished by scriptural writers for the sake of emphasis, or even because of their own unbelief in or incomprehension of the subtler workings of spirit. Nevertheless, no one today was present for these past events. Neither is nature an iron block of determinism, where events are invariably caused in a certain way. Rather, there is a "usual way" in which events are encountered. And that way determines the customary, even the modern scientific, view of the world. So the miracle of Jesus walking on water and Peter attempting to do so can be understood as having explicitly occurred as described. For causal relations are not cast in iron, no matter how regular, and therefore highly probable, they may be in ordinary experience. Or the reported miracle can be accepted as a deliberately descriptive means of stressing the importance of faith. In the latter case, something extraordinary would certainly have taken place. But it need not have been as dramatic as in the narrative. The writer of this book is inclined to the latter view. The advantage of this viewpoint is that it places greater weight on a transformation of character and less on an attitude of credulousness.)

Why do you also transgress the commandment of God by your tradition? For God commanded, saying, Honor your father and mother: and, He that curses father or mother, let him die the death. But you say, Whoever shall say to his father or his mother, It is a gift, by whatever you might be profited by me; And honor not his father or his mother, he shall be free. Thus have you made the commandment of God of none effect by your tradition. You hypocrites, well did Esaias prophesy of you, saying, This people draws nigh to me with their mouth, and honors me with their lips; but their heart is far from me. But in vain they do worship me, teaching for doctrines the commandments of men.

Most people occasionally falsify the truth, sometimes knowingly, more often inadvertently. A few continually and deliberately falsify it in order to sway others by deception. And a great many people, either out of naiveté or an underlying indifference, adhere to the falsifications which have been made. Yet the truth is simple and can be recognized by the fact that it comes directly from the heart. The master plan of the material world is cunning, not wisdom. It is by this means that falsifiers think up schemes to entrap people's minds, so that they may control them through their beliefs. And, when called into question, their deceptions are generally presented as being made for the sake of maintaining moral conformity and social harmony. But this kind of moral conformity, and the social harmony which depends upon it, has no enduring value and eventually leads to the dissolution which is the universal character of the material order. There is only one path to peace and harmony. It is to draw near to God, which is to live in the spirit. For God is spirit, the principle of unity, harmony, and peace. So each person engaging in a life of the spirit is the only means of creating a lasting social harmony. Whereas to draw near to material symbols and symbolic acts, which presume to indirectly represent the inherent unity of spirit, is to submit to the characteristic divisiveness of material experience.

Hear, and understand: Not that which goes into the mouth defiles a man; but that which comes out of the mouth, this defiles a man.

What goes into the mouth affects the body. It provides material sustenance for a material body. But what comes out of the mouth comes from thought, which, in varying degrees, expresses spirit. For the human mind is an instrument employing both spirit and matter, as it is composed of both. Thus a person cannot think without using material images for her thoughts. But her thoughts are themselves made possible by spirit. And they can, if so chosen, be made to reflect the experience of spirit. Of course, not all material thoughts defile a person. But those which are governed by material motives can, when they are applied to moral purposes. So what comes out of the mouth may come either from the spirit or from a preoccupation with material things. For this reason, it may either bless or curse a person.

Then came his disciples, and said unto him, Know you that the Pharisees were offended, after they heard this saying? But he answered and said, Every plant, which my heavenly Father has not planted, shall be rooted up. Let them alone: they be blind leaders of the blind. And if the blind lead the blind, both shall fall into the ditch.

The Pharisees have submitted to the darkness of their minds. And those who follow them do the same. (Nevertheless, the darkened, materially entrapped character of these minds, and any others like them, will be transformed by the spirit when the proper time comes. For the darkness and confusion will be taken away.)

And Jesus said, Are you also yet without understanding? Do not you yet understand, that whatever enters in at the mouth goes into the belly, and is cast out into the draught? But those things which proceed out of the mouth come forth from the heart; and they defile the man. For out of the heart proceed evil thoughts, murders, adulteries, fornications, thefts, false witness, blasphemies: These are the things which defile a man: but to eat with unwashed hands defiles not a man.

The explanation is the same as that following the presentation of the parable above. In addition, the statement is added that external practices have no bearing in the matter. It is not rituals but attitudes which cleanse the mind and heart.

I am not sent but to the lost sheep of the house of Israel. It is not meet to take the children's bread, and to cast it to dogs.

This emphasizes Jesus' principal mission. It is those for whom temple religion offers so little who have an immediate need of his teaching and who will most readily understand him. But in time his sense of mission seems to have broadened beyond this. For he not only brought comfort to the disenfranchised. He directly challenged the temple authority. He did this because he realized that there could be no compromise between the inner spirit and outer practice. The genuine reality is spirit. And it must shine forth as the predominant truth.

O woman, great is your faith: be it to you even as you will.

Nevertheless, in spite of what is said in the above quote, it is an open heart which is the fundamental focus of his mission. This is what clearly demonstrates that his mission was ultimately universal. It will in time affect every nation on earth, but not under doctrine. Rather, it will penetrate and infuse itself into the various manners of belief, lifting the members of each separate dispensation into the complete freedom of spirit. Some have not far to go in this understanding. Others do. In either case, Jesus' teachings are not the seeds of a new religion. They point to an understanding of what human beings truly are.

When it is evening, you say, It will be fair weather: for the sky is red. And in the morning, It will be foul weather today: for the sky is red and lowering. O you hypocrites, you can discern the face of the sky; but can you not discern the signs of the times?

Put aside your preoccupation with material things and material reasoning. An understanding and recognition of the things of the spirit comes from the spirit. And these are more important. A person does not have to search far to find the ground of himself. It is closer to him than the beating of his own heart. It is in his motivation and thinking, even when this is misdirected by material divisiveness. For every person seeks to assert his own enduring character. But this quality is not to be found in material considerations. Rather, it is in spirit. This is why it is so easy for a person to recognize the material divisiveness of his seeing and thinking, to understand how it originates, and to be able to set it aside and find unity within himself.

Take heed and beware of the leaven of the Pharisees and of the Sadducees.

Wrong thinking, worldly and material thinking, can spread through the mind and overcome it. In such a case, the things of the spirit can have no entrance. This wrong thinking can creep in anywhere, no matter how spiritual the claim. The only way to recognize it is by its unspiritual results.

And Simon Peter answered and said, You are the Christ, the Son of the living God. And Jesus answered and said to him, Blessed are you, Simon Bar-jona: for flesh and blood have not revealed it to you, but my Father which is in heaven. And I say also to you, That you are Peter, and upon this rock I will build my church; and the gates of hell shall not prevail against it. And I will give to you the keys of the kingdom of heaven: and whatever you shall bind on earth shall be bound in heaven: and whatever you shall loose on earth shall be loosed in heaven.

Peter sees that Jesus lives wholly in the spirit. This has been shown to him by the spirit within him. And it is this kind of opening of the heart and mind to the things of the spirit which will grow among humanity. Nothing can prevent it. In that spiritual condition the desires, thoughts, and acts of a person, such as Peter, are in right accord with both spiritual and material experience. This is the rock of Peter's faith and the faith of all people, out of which the domain of spirit will be built among them. This domain of spirit involves being in right accord with both spiritual and material experience. And to be in a right accord with both spiritual and material experience is to will what is right both in the spiritual and in the material realms of experience. It is to be in harmony with one's existence. The keys of the kingdom of heaven are this spiritual harmony. For, where such harmony exists, whatever the mind of a spiritual person should bind or loose in the material is already bound or loosed in the spirit.

Then said Jesus to his disciples, If any man will come after me, let him deny himself, and take up his cross, and follow me. For whoever will save his life shall lose it: and whoever will lose his life for my sake shall find it. For what is a man profited, if he shall gain the whole world, and lose his own soul? or what shall a man give in exchange for his soul? For the Son of man

63

shall come in the glory of his Father with his angels; and then he shall reward every man according to his works. Verily I say to you, There be some standing here, which shall not taste of death, till they see the Son of man coming in his kingdom.

If any person will live the spiritual life, she must turn away from her material self and the interests and preoccupations which concern that self. She must do this in order to take on the life of spirit. Whoever will cling to her material life will lose the spiritual life. And whoever will cling to the spiritual life will preserve it. Both the spiritual and the material will then be preserved, the spiritual first. For it is the spirit which endures, not the material. For this reason, comparatively little is gained if a person clings to the material life in preference to the spiritual. She loses her very person. What is more valuable than her essential character, her true self? A transformation of all people to the spirit will come. Some will go quietly into spiritual life and some with varying degrees of notable activity. Each will find her place and the level of comfort she needs. It is better for a person's own peace of mind to be early rather than late in the transformation. So there are some, recognizing this, who even now will make the transition.

If you have faith as a grain of mustard seed, you shall say to this mountain, Remove hence to yonder place; and it shall remove; and nothing shall be impossible unto you.

Faith, which is life in the spirit, is transformative. Even in the simplest heart its effect is overwhelming. Things which seemed impossible will be of little concern. For the mind and heart have found a way to set things right between themselves and the details of living.

What think you, Simon? of whom do the kings of the earth take custom or tribute? of their own children, or of strangers? Peter says to him, Of strangers. Jesus says to him, Then are the children free. Notwithstanding, lest we should offend them, go you to the sea, and cast a hook, and take up the fish that first comes up; and when you have opened his mouth, you shall find a piece of money: that take, and give to them for me and you.

Taxation is a material concern. It does not pertain to the sons of man, who are self-acknowledged sons of God. They are of the spirit and are free of material constraints. Nevertheless, the concerns of the material world must be met where the circumstances of material life demand them. So meet those concerns willingly.

Verily I say to you, Except you be converted, and become as little children, you shall not enter into the kingdom of heaven. Whoever therefore shall humble himself as this little child, the same is greatest in the kingdom of heaven. And whoever shall receive one such little child in my name receives me. But whoever shall offend one of these little ones which believe in me, it were better for him that a millstone were hanged about his neck, and that he were drowned in the depth of the sea.

To enter into a life of the spirit, a person must put aside the reasonings developed from and for the purpose of coping with material concerns. He must become open and free in spirit like a child. In the realm of spirit such an attitude is paramount. It defines the life of spirit and makes it possible. To accept another person who has made this transition is to accept what Jesus represents. To go against such a person is to go against the life of spirit. Nothing can be worse than a material life with no spiritual possibility.

Woe to the world because of offences! for it must needs be that offences come; but woe to that man by whom the offence comes! Wherefore if your hand or your foot offends you, cut them off, and cast them from you: it is better for you to enter into life halt or maimed, rather than having two hands or two feet to be cast into everlasting fire. And if your eye offends you, pluck it out, and cast it from you: it is better for you to enter into life with one eye, rather than having two eyes to be cast into hell fire.

While the world is under the governance of materially minded people, the life of the spirit will be little regarded. But each materially minded person loses much. For she is self-condemned to that which brings no comfort. So, if some aspect of your life cuts you off from the spirit, distance yourself from it. It is better to be so distanced than to suffer the anguish of a life lived denying the spirit. For that anguish is present, even when it is not recognized that the anguish is unnecessary.

Take heed that you despise not one of these little ones; for I say to you, That in heaven their angels do always behold the face of my Father which is in heaven. For the Son of man is come to save that which was lost.

Do not look down on those of a spiritual character, though they may seem simple to you. For they have embraced the most profound and deepest meaning of life. And their spirits are turned inward towards God. These are the ones the Son of man has come to set free. He has come to restore the human spirit to its proper mooring in universal spirit.

How think you? if a man has a hundred sheep, and one of them be gone astray, does he not leave the ninety and nine, and go into the mountains, and seek that which is gone astray? And if so be that he find it, verily I say to you, he rejoices more of that sheep, than of the ninety and nine which went not astray. Even so it is not the will of your Father which is in heaven, that one of these little ones should perish.

It is not in the nature of the spirit to accept the final loss of anyone.

Moreover if your brother shall trespass against you, go and tell him his fault between you and him alone: if he shall hear you, you have gained your brother. But if he will not hear you, then take with you one or two more, that in the mouth of two or three witnesses every word may be established. And if he shall neglect to hear them, tell it to the church: but if he neglect to hear the church, let him be to you as an heathen man and a publican.

Try sincerely to live in honest harmony with others. But if nothing will change another person, then accept his decision and go on without him.

Verily I say to you, Whatever you shall bind on earth shall be bound in heaven: and whatever you shall loose on earth shall be loosed in heaven.

This was previously said to Peter. Now it is being generalized. This close accord of a person with both the spirit and the material, where they are brought into harmony with one another within that person, comes only through the spirit.

Again I say to you, That if two of you shall agree on earth as touching any thing that they shall ask, it shall be done for them of my Father which is in heaven. For where two or three are gathered together in my name, there am I in the midst of them.

Where the mind is in harmony with the spirit, and this in harmony with others of like character, there is perfect accord in the spirit. And what is desired in such a manner—that is, in the manner of the spirit (not the material)—will be.

Then came Peter to him, and said, Lord, how often shall my brother sin against me, and I forgive him? till seven times? Jesus said to him, I say not to you, Until seven times: but, Until seventy times seven. Therefore is the kingdom of heaven likened to a certain king, which would take account of his servants. And when he had begun to reckon, one was brought to him, which owed him ten thousand talents. But forasmuch as he had not to pay, his lord commanded him to be sold, and his wife, and children, and all that he had, and payment to be made. The servant therefore fell down, and worshipped him, saying, Lord, have patience with me, and I will pay you all. Then the lord of that servant was moved with compassion, and loosed him, and forgave him the debt. But the same servant went out, and found one of his fellow servants, which owed him a hundred pence: and he laid hands on him, and took him by the throat, saying, Pay me that you owe. And his fellow servant fell down at his feet, and besought him, saying, Have patience with me, and I will pay you all. And he would not: but went and cast him into prison, till he should pay the debt. So when his fellow servants saw what was done, they were very sorry, and came and told their lord all that was done. Then his lord, after that he had called him, said to him, O you wicked servant, I forgave you all that debt, because you desired me to: Should not you also have had compassion on your fellow servant, even as I had pity on you? And his lord was wroth, and delivered him to the tormentors, till he should pay all that was due to him. So likewise shall my heavenly Father do also to you, if you from your hearts forgive not every one his brother their trespasses.

Non-forgiveness arises either from a fear of repeated offense or from the sense of an offended ego and thus a fear that the offended person will suffer a diminished psychological importance in the minds of others. In either case, these are the ways of a material perspective. Since Jesus taught the kingdom of spiritual-mindedness and not the state of material-mindedness, he emphasized the natural equanimity of spirit. A spiritual state of mind entertains a larger view, which seeks to understand by seeing all sides of an issue rather than to condemn. It is a state neither presently universally achieved nor fully achievable within material circumstances. Only in the completeness of unrestricted spiritual life can it be realized without exception. But, if people in this life were all to turn toward such a spiritually centered state of mind, a near approximation could be arrived at. At any rate, there would be much less troubling of the mind in the life of each person.

Have you not read, that he which made them at the beginning made them male and female, And said, For this cause shall a man leave father and mother, and shall cleave to his wife: and they twain shall be one flesh? Wherefore they are no more twain, but one flesh. What therefore God has joined together, let not man put asunder. They said to him, Why did Moses then command to give a writing of divorcement, and to put her away? He said to them, Moses because of the hardness of your hearts suffered you to put away your wives: but from the beginning it was not so. And I say to you, Whoever shall put away his wife, except it be for fornication, and shall marry another, commits adultery: and whoever marries her which is put away does commit adultery. His disciples said to him, If the case of the man be so with his wife, it is not good to marry. But he said to them, All men cannot receive this saying, save they to whom it is given. For there are some eunuchs, which were so born from their mother's womb: and there are some eunuchs, which were made eunuchs of men: and there be eunuchs, which have made themselves eunuchs for the kingdom of heaven's sake. He that is able to receive it, let him receive it.

In the true way, a man and a woman should be joined in such a manner that theirs is a meeting of minds and hearts. They become one in spirit. It is not a matter of their becoming the same mind or heart. They are individuals, even in the spirit. But it is a condition of their functioning as one mind and heart, where they are harmonized in life's purpose with another. It is this sharing of purpose which makes them one. For the act of marriage is a reflection of the one universal spirit. Universal spirit is universal consciousness. It is this one consciousness which gives awareness, and therefore life, to each person. And it is the same universal spirit which brings meaning separately to both partners, uniting that meaning into one in their union. Thus, being grounded in this unity of spirit, the union of the two people expresses the indivisibility of spirit. So, since it partakes of the character of spirit, it cannot be broken. For the one purpose in spirit which is shared by the two people, however differently arranged in their two minds, is the one purpose of spirit. To break this bond is to tear that which is one into two parts, a contradiction of the character of spirit. Having committed this act, the mind and heart of each person is returned to a material perspective, where there is division, competition, and enmity. This is an adulteration of the soul. For their union had made them one. And now they are each less than whole. So anyone subsequently joined to either fragmented part becomes a party to that adulteration. However, this applies only to those people who seek a union with one another. Not all people are destined to marry. Some people are so filled with spiritual purpose, they find fulfilment in spirit alone. These people are the spiritual eunuchs.

71

Suffer little children, and forbid them not, to come to me: for of such is the kingdom of heaven.

Here again is an emphasis on the open-minded, open-hearted innocence of small children. Such an attitude is necessary to enter into the condition of spiritual-mindedness.

Why call you me good? there is none good but one, that is, God: but if you will enter into life, keep the commandments.

The spirit is good, not the person. God is spirit. Jesus makes it clear that this distinction applies to himself as well. It is the spirit in him which is good. Any person, including Jesus, is good only inasmuch as the spirit operates within him. The commandments should be adhered to because they are an expression of spiritual unity, where there is no place for distrust, division, enmity, and disharmony. So to live in the spirit demands a respect for the commandments. However, this does not mean that keeping the commandments alone is equivalent to living in the spirit. It is conceivable that a person can obey the letter of the law coldly from a material perspective. Many do. But, as Jesus says elsewhere, these are the ones whom the spirit will not recognize.

You shall do no murder, You shalt not commit adultery, You shall not steal, You shall not bear false witness, Honor your father and your mother: and, You shall love your neighbour as yourself.

All these commands but the last have to do with trust. For a harmonious society to exist, one person must be able to trust another not to murder her, not to commit adultery against her, not to steal from her, and not to bear false witness against her. In addition to these society-building rules, she should not be ungrateful to those who have been assigned by spirit as the instruments of bringing her into life and of her early care and instruction. For her to betray their trust is unconscionable. The last commandment is, in fact, the reason for all the others. For in the spirit all are one. And that unity occasions respect, one for another. This respect is love. But it is not necessarily an emotion. Emotions cannot be extended universally. For emotions require personal involvement. Even empathy can only be applied to what is imagined in some way to be a personal involvement. Respect, on the other hand, can and should be exercised without any such restrictions.

If you will be perfect, go and sell that which you have, and give to the poor, and you shall have treasure in heaven: and come and follow me.

If you want to enter fully into the life of the spirit, separate yourself from your material interests and let your possessions help those who need them most. In the spirit, where there is no division, enmity, suffering, and death, there is a life of peace and harmony. Even in this material frame of existence, there can be an access to and understanding of this more enduring reality. So come and be as I am.

Verily I say to you, That a rich man shall hardly enter into the kingdom of heaven. And again I say to you, It is easier for a camel to go through the eye of a needle, than for a rich man to enter into the kingdom of God.

To have wealth is to desire to maintain it and perhaps increase it. In this there is worry that the wealth cannot be maintained, hope that it might be increased, and opposition toward those who would reduce it or prevent its increase. The greatest hope is that wealth can bring peace of mind. It does not. Instead, a person must always keep up his guard and never relax his vigilance, lest the wealth slip away from him and dissipate into the hands of others. These preoccupations are material concerns. And they leave little room for spiritual life. Yet, because of the immediacy of material experience and the sense of urgency it produces, such concerns are hard to overcome. So it is nearly impossible for a rich person to become spiritually-minded. To do so, he would have to let go of what he believes is so important in sustaining him.

When his disciples heard it, they were exceedingly amazed, saying, Who then can be saved? But Jesus beheld them, and said to them, With men this is impossible; but with God all things are possible.

The disciples were amazed because they knew that no one can completely neglect material concerns. How could they continue to answer to their physical needs, yet seek to become absorbed in the spiritual? But Jesus assured them that the spirit is not passive. It will awaken and transform those who are willing and in time even those who are not willing. The transformation will occur even in the midst of material concerns.

Verily I say to you, That you which have followed me, in the regeneration when the Son of man shall sit in the throne of his glory, you also shall sit upon twelve thrones, judging the twelve tribes of Israel. And every one that has forsaken houses, or brethren, or sisters, or father, or mother, or wife, or children, or lands, for my name's sake, shall receive an hundredfold, and shall inherit everlasting life. But many that are first shall be last; and the last shall be first.

Those who follow the example of Jesus, and are able to put spirit above all concerns, will be like kings in their spiritual state, filled with wisdom and understanding of their fellow beings. In other words, the sons of God which they truly are, though this should initially be unbeknownst to them, will transform them into the sons of man they are meant to be. For each person will become a fully realized son of God *in* a man. That is, she will become a person who is a son of God who knows she is a son of God. In that condition, no person will be greater than another. For in the spirit all are one, except in individual self-awareness. So there is no overlordship. But some will have sought a greater depth of spiritual understanding, since it is their nature to do so. In this they will excel. But there will be no jealousy among those who do not have this inclination. Each person has her special place. They are all peacemakers who desire equanimity and harmony. And among them are seekers after truth who long for a fuller understanding.

For the kingdom of heaven is like a man that is a householder, which went out early in the morning to hire laborers into his vineyard. And when he had agreed with the laborers for a penny a day, he sent them into his vineyard. And he went out about the third hour, and saw others standing idle in the marketplace, And said to them; Go you also into the vineyard, and whatever is right I will give you. And they went their way. Again he went out about the sixth and ninth hour, and did likewise. And about the eleventh hour he went out, and found others standing idle, and said to them, Why stand you here all the day idle? They said to him, Because no man has hired us. He said to them, Go you also into the vineyard; and whatever is right, that shall you receive. So when even was come, the lord of the vineyard said to his steward, Call the laborers, and give them their hire, beginning from the last to the first. And when they came that were hired about the eleventh hour, they received every man a penny. But when the first came, they supposed that they should have received more; and they likewise received every man a penny. And when they had received it, they murmured against the goodman of the house, Saying, These last have wrought but one hour, and you have made them equal to us, which have borne the burden and heat of the day. But he answered one of them, and said, Friend, I do you no wrong: did not you agree with me for a penny? Take that yours is, and go your way: I will give to this last, even as to you. Is it not lawful for me to do what I will with my own? Is your eye evil, because I am good? So the last shall be first, and the first last: for many be called, but few chosen.

The notable fact in the parable is that the last and the first are equal in pay, though their labor is not equal. This gives a special meaning to the concept of the last being first and the first last. It means they are all one. They are equal in the spirit. The spirit beckons many and they respond, some quickly, some later. But what matters is that they respond. Nevertheless, it is true that some will live and act more deeply in the spirit in certain respects than others because they do not all respond in the same way. For they are not identical persons and are not given the same purpose. Thus it will seem as if some labor more. But this does not make them better than others. They are simply different. They are led from within themselves to labor more. In other words, there should be an appreciation of the fact that people are individuals. No reward is needed for a person being who he is. Nor is there any penalty for a person being who he is.

Then came to him the mother of Zebedee's children with her sons, worshipping him, and desiring a certain thing of him. And he said to her, What will you? She said to him, Grant that these my two sons may sit, the one on your right hand, and the other on the left, in your kingdom. But Jesus answered and said, You know not what you ask. Are you able to drink of the cup that I shall drink of, and to be baptized with the baptism that I am baptized with? They said to him, We are able. And he said to them, You shall drink indeed of my cup, and be baptized with the baptism that I am baptized with: but to sit on my right hand, and on my left, is not mine to give, but it shall be given to them for whom it is prepared of my Father.

In an age opposing spiritual things, a life in the spirit can be difficult. For it involves alienation toward accustomed attitudes and ways: a complete change of mind-set. Many will shun, misunderstand, or ridicule the one who adopts such a way of life.

So this cup can be bitter, the baptism not easily sought for. Nevertheless, this is the task. And life in the spirit is the goal. Those who take on this task are fully realized sons of God. But no son of God, including Jesus, knows the mind of spirit. He can find only his own purpose in the spirit. Where this leads is not up to him. It is where the spirit leads. In other words, it is where his individual character takes him, once his mind is transformed into an understanding of life in the spirit.

You know that the princes of the Gentiles exercise dominion over them, and they that are great exercise authority upon them. But it shall not be so among you: but whoever will be great among you, let him be your minister; And whoever will be chief among you, let him be your servant: Even as the Son of man came not to be ministered to, but to minister, and to give his life a ransom for many.

Materially-minded people, in their thirst for power and precedence, create hierarchies of authority among themselves. This is in compensation for the material limitation they experience in themselves. But in the spirit, there is no material limitation. All are united in the oneness of spirit. They remain individuals, but without a sense of alienation from one another. So there can be no hierarchy in the spirit. That is why Jesus came to teach the spiritual truth and to give his life for it, so that many would learn of and be drawn to the spirit. Jesus often mentions the fact that he "came" to do such-and-such. What does this mean? Does it mean that he existed beforetime and accepted this assignment? It both does and does not mean this. For time is a condition of material limitation. So there is no time in the spirit, except where spirit makes it a local condition, as is the case in the present material realm. Jesus is simply Jesus, as every other person is simply who he or she is. Each person has a spiritual character to be discovered and brought to fruition in this life, if the person seeks to do so. Jesus lived full of a consciousness of the spirit. So much so, it was the all-in-all to him. This he freely chose, as it was his character to do so. He could have done otherwise (witness the agonizing prayer in the Garden of Gethsemane). But his already attained fullness in the spirit made that unlikely.

It is written, My house shall be called the house of prayer; but you have made it a den of thieves.

In their material interest, people, including those in religious authority, have subverted the meaning and purpose of spirit. The money-changing and sale of birds for sacrifice were being done for profit. And this was taking place on the temple grounds. Sacrifice itself was a barbaric symbol of submission to God. It had been taken over from ancient and surrounding influences. For this reason it was incorporated into religious practice and tolerated. But the prophets inveighed against it: "I will have mercy, and not sacrifice." In other words: I will have acts of a spiritual mind and heart, not the material symbols which have been substituted in their place. Profiting from this was a step even further away from the spirit. It clearly demonstrated the problem which was likely to arise from such material symbols. One step into material-mindedness eventually leads into an even more egregious material-mindedness. For the first time, Jesus directly took on the maladjusted temple religion itself. In doing so, he was perceived as threatening the power structure of the materially-minded religious authority.

79

And when the chief priests and scribes saw the wonderful things that he did, and the children crying in the temple, and saying, Hosanna to the Son of David; they were sore displeased, And said to him, Hear you what these say? And Jesus said to them, Yes; have you never read, Out of the mouth of babes and sucklings you have perfected praise?

From the original, uncorrupted heart of humankind comes spiritual recognition and joy. It does not depend upon human authority.

And when he saw a fig tree in the way, he came to it, and found nothing thereon, but leaves only, and said to it, Let no fruit grow on you henceforward for ever. And presently the fig tree withered away.

Life in the spirit bears fruit in a person's character and acts. Where there is no such fruit, the life of the spirit has been smothered by other concerns. So it cannot bear spiritual fruit. And, if this condition remains, the spirit, which is life, will die within that person. The fig tree was withered away because, having no fruit, it had no purpose in existing.

And when the disciples saw it, they marvelled, saying, How soon is the fig tree withered away! Jesus answered and said to them, Verily I say to you, If you have faith, and doubt not, you shall not only do this which is done to the fig tree, but also if you shall say to this mountain, Be you removed, and be you cast into the sea; it shall be done. And all things, whatever you shall ask in prayer, believing, you shall receive.

All things are possible in the spirit. But it should be remembered that a life in the spirit is a complete change of mind-set. So in a spiritual mind-set what is asked for is in accord with spirit. That is why the statement, "whatever you shall ask *in prayer*, believing, you shall receive." What is not meant by this teaching is that, if a person wants to accomplish something extraordinary out of his own vanity, it will happen. Spiritual acts cannot originate in material motives.

And when he was come into the temple, the chief priests and the elders of the people came to him as he was teaching, and said, By what authority do you these things? and who gave you this authority? And Jesus answered and said to them, I also will ask you one thing, which if you tell me, I in like wise will tell you by what authority I do these things. The baptism of John, whence was it? from heaven, or of men? And they reasoned with themselves, saying, If we shall say, From heaven; he will say to us, Why did you not then believe him? But if we shall say, Of men; we fear the people; for all hold John as a prophet. And they answered Jesus, and said, We cannot tell. And he said to them, Neither tell I you by what authority I do these things. But what think you? A certain man had two sons; and he came to the first, and said, Son, go work to day in my vineyard. He answered and said, I will not: but afterward he repented, and went. And he came to the second, and said likewise. And he answered and said, I go, sir: and went not. Whether of them twain did the will of his father? They said to him, The first. Jesus said to them, Verily I say to you, That the publicans and the harlots go into the kingdom of God before you. For John came to you in the way of righteousness, and you believed him not: but the publicans and the harlots believed him: and you, when you had seen it, repented not afterward, that you might believe him. Hear another parable: There was a certain householder, which planted a vineyard, and hedged it round about, and dug a winepress in it, and built a tower, and let it out to husbandmen, and went into a far country: And when the time of the fruit drew near, he sent his servants to the husbandmen, that they might receive the fruits of it. And the husbandmen took his servants, and beat one, and killed another, and stoned another. Again, he sent other servants more than the first: and they did to them likewise. But last of all he sent to them his son, saying, They will reverence my son. But when the husbandmen saw the son, they said among themselves, This is the heir; come, let us kill him, and let us seize on his inheritance. And they caught him, and cast him out of the vineyard, and slew him. When the lord therefore of the vineyard cometh, what will he do to those husbandmen? They said to him, He will miserably destroy those wicked men, and will let out his vineyard to other husbandmen, which shall render him the fruits in their seasons. Jesus said to them, Did you never read in the scriptures, The stone which the builders rejected, the same is become the head of the corner: this is the Lord's doing, and it is marvellous in our eyes? Therefore say I to you, The kingdom of God shall be taken from you, and given to a nation bringing forth the fruits thereof. And whoever shall fall on this stone shall be broken: but on whomever it shall fall, it will grind him to powder.

Those who could not, or would not, recognize where John's spiritual insight came from would have no positive use for Jesus' message. On the other hand, those who accept and understand matters of the spirit will find their place in the spirit. But the others, regardless of their material lineage or claims, will not. As they ignore or reject the spirit, they will reject others of the spirit. Thus teachers of the spirit who come to them will be rejected. This includes even the purest of those teachers, the one most fully embedded in the spirit. This is Jesus. So his ministry is a turning point. So full and so clear is the message he represents that to reject it or subvert it is to turn away from the spirit once and for all. This, of course, means that the spirit is then turned irrevocably away from those who turn away from it. For it is a reciprocal relationship. As one thing draws apart from another, they are both placed at a greater distance from one another. For this reason, Jesus will either be the means of change in people, breaking their old frame of mind and causing a complete turnabout in their thinking. Or they will reject him and destroy their own spiritual life by this means.

The kingdom of heaven is like a certain king, which made a marriage for his son, And sent forth his servants to call them that were bidden to the wedding: and they would not come. Again, he sent forth other servants, saying, Tell them which are bidden, Behold, I have prepared my dinner: my oxen and my fatlings are killed, and all things are ready: come to the marriage. But they made light of it, and went their ways, one to his farm, another to his merchandise: And the remnant took his servants, and entreated them spitefully, and slew them. But when the king heard thereof, he was wroth: and he sent forth his armies, and destroyed those murderers, and burned up their city. Then said he to his servants, The wedding is ready, but they which were bidden were not worthy. Go you therefore into the highways, and as many as you shall find, bid to the marriage. So those servants went out into the highways, and gathered together all as many as they found, both bad and good: and the wedding was furnished with guests. And when the king came in to see the guests, he saw there a man which had not on a wedding garment: And he said to him, Friend, how came you in hither not having a wedding garment? And he was speechless. Then said the king to the servants, Bind him hand and foot, and take him away, and cast him into outer darkness; there shall be weeping and gnashing of teeth. For many are called, but few are chosen.

The first-called guests, because of their set doctrines, practices, and established power structure (like those of the elders and priests of the temple), are so embedded in a material mind-set that they cannot accept a new, different, and more complete insight into spiritual matters, especially one which leads away from what they have already invested themselves in. So other guests must be called, openly and freely. It does not matter who they are or what they have done, if they will accept the new vision. But some come unprepared nevertheless, not having turned their minds and hearts toward the spirit. As a result, neither have they in any way put on even the most obvious behavioral garments of the new teaching. Thus they stand out noticeably as being alien to it. They are therefore excluded from the life of the spirit and left in the material world of divisions, enmity, and bitter regrets.

Render therefore to Caesar the things which are Caesar's; and to God the things that are God's.

In this life, material concerns cannot be completely done away with. But they should not prevent the spiritual transformation of a person's life and attitudes. Material concerns will then be looked after from a spiritual frame of mind.

[Concerning the woman with seven sequential husbands, as to whom she would be married to in the afterlife] You do err, not knowing the scriptures, nor the power of God. For in the resurrection they neither marry, nor are given in marriage, but are as the angels of God in heaven.

In the material realm, there is isolated individual consciousness and intelligence. But in the immaterial realm the various human experiences of consciousness are united in one universal consciousness, thus losing their sense of isolation while remaining capable of continuing in their individuality. In addition, since reason is a product of material limitation, spiritual intelligences are not in the material sense rational. They transcend the rational, thus being capable of understanding more than what the rational encompasses. For each spiritualized human being knows that she is ultimately an expression of one universal spirit, the mind of which is completely unknown to a material intelligence (and only partially known to a spiritual intelligence like herself). In this spiritualized realm, marriage does not exist, since marriage is founded upon sexual reproduction and an experience of emotional and intellectual isolation which create a special need for bonding with another person to relieve that isolation. These expressions of an absolute material limitation do not pertain to the spiritual environment, since there is greater connectivity in the community of spiritual oneness. There is also no problem of a limited duration (a time-bound life-span), since an individual spiritual mind's grounding in timeless universal spirit is then understood. Rather, absolute time-bound limitation is a strictly material experience. Accordingly, since sexual reproduction has to do with isolated individual existences, it is these existences which appear to undergo a limited duration in the material sphere. Hence the experience of death. Emotional isolation is present for the same reason, resulting, as it does, from an inability to see beyond the confines of one materially oriented mind.

But as touching the resurrection of the dead, have you not read that which was spoken to you by God, saying, I am the God of Abraham, and the God of Isaac, and the God of Jacob? God is not the God of the dead, but of the living.

Spiritual life is eternal. Only the material body is shed, like hair or fingernails. It is as though one were confined within a camera box and could only see the world through a tiny aperture. When the camera box falls away, all is seen. Likewise, the suffering undergone in material life, though terrible, is similar to the memory of birth pains after the delivery of a child. In the subsequent joy, the pains are forgotten.

You shall love the Lord your God with all your heart, and with all your soul, and with all your mind. This is the first and great commandment. And the second is like it, You shall love your neighbour as yourself. On these two commandments hang all the law and the prophets.

A person must be immersed entirely in the life of the spirit and fully devoted to it. There can be no divided loyalty or state of mind. Material existence must flow from the spirit (which it truly does) and not be alternate to it. Also, living in the spirit, each person should have a high regard and respect for all other human beings. This is not agape, since agape implies emotional love. Emotional love is contingent upon an intimate knowledge or empathy for the person. Since it requires the application of imagination to persons either known or known about in some concrete way, this cannot be made universal in material life. Rather, it is respect which must rise to a universal application. This respect comes not from a specific knowledge of individual persons, but from an awareness that each person, whatever that person's circumstances or attitudes, is a son of God. When viewed in this light, it can be seen that all the commandments, as well as the expressions of the prophets, concern these two practices because they are inevitably either about closeness to the spirit or about maintaining a relationship of trust and respect with other people.

While the Pharisees were gathered together, Jesus asked them, Saying, What think you of Christ? whose son is he? They said to him, The Son of David. He said to them, How then does David in spirit call him Lord, saying, The LORD said to my

Lord, Sit you on my right hand, till I make your enemies your footstool? If David then call him Lord, how is he his son?

Whose son is the Christ? If he is the Christ, he is fully immersed in and expressive of spirit. In other words, he is spirit. And spirit has no material lineage.

But be not you called Rabbi: for one is your Master, even Christ; and all you are brethren. And call no man your father upon the earth: for one is your Father, which is in heaven. Neither be you called masters: for one is your Master, even Christ. But he that is greatest among you shall be your servant. And whosoever shall exalt himself shall be abased; and he that shall humble himself shall be exalted.

There is only one teacher: him through whom the life and understanding of the spirit is expressed (in this case, Jesus). There is only one creator and sustainer of mankind. This is the spirit. Any material cause, genetic or otherwise, belongs to the appearances of the material realm. But everything comes from the spirit. True causation is in the spirit from which all things emanate. It is not in what appear to be the material relations of cause and effect. So all people are one in the spirit and should behave accordingly. To set oneself above others in the material realm is to draw away from spirit. Its consequence is the anguish of that separation. But to be drawn into the spirit is to be consciously filled with the source of all things.

Woe to you, scribes and Pharisees, hypocrites! for you pay tithe of mint and anise and cumin, and have omitted the weightier matters of the law, judgment, mercy, and faith: these ought you to have done, and not to leave the other undone. You blind guides, which strain at a gnat, and swallow a camel. Woe to you, scribes and Pharisees, hypocrites! for you make clean the outside of the cup and of the platter, but within they are full of extortion and excess. You blind Pharisee, cleanse first that which is within the cup and platter, that the outside of them may be clean also. Woe to you, scribes and Pharisees, hypocrites! for you are like whitened sepulchres, which indeed appear beautiful outward, but are within full of dead men's bones, and of all uncleanness. Even so you also outwardly appear righteous to men, but within you are full of hypocrisy and iniquity.

The things of the spirit are justice, sincerity, trustworthiness, concern for others, and the strength and confidence of person that comes from a life fully invested in the spirit. The things of the material are division, cunning, deceit, self-serving attitudes, and a life expressing fear of one's own personal limitations. Those who value their worldly position more than their true character, or those who act as if they believe the material is all there is, will subvert the spiritual and lead others away from it. They will emphasize trivial outward observances over an inward, character-elevating behavior. In doing this they appear to be what they are not. They appear spiritual and whole in demeanor, but are darkness and division within. For they see and care for nothing but their limited selves.

[Jesus addresses Jerusalem, and thus Jewish officialdom, from his spiritual state of mind.] O Jerusalem, Jerusalem, you that kill the prophets, and stone them which are sent to you, how often would I have gathered your children together, even as a

*hen gathers her chickens under her wings, and you would not!
Behold, your house is left to you desolate. For I say to you,
You shall not see me henceforth, till you shall say, Blessed is
he that comes in the name of the Lord.*

Universal spirit, God, would bring all the people together in
peace and harmony and without a rigid political/religious
hierarchy based on the material will. But the hierarchy and their
followers will not have it. So they are without spirit and will not
see it again until the whole of humanity is brought within it.

*Wherefore if they shall say to you, Behold, he is in the desert;
go not forth: behold, he is in the secret chambers; believe it
not. For as the lightning comes out of the east, and shines even
to the west; so shall also the coming of the Son of man be.*

The spiritual transformation of humankind is not a matter of
place. It is a transformation from within. And it will be
immediate and plain enough to all who are transformed.

*Verily I say to you, This generation shall not pass, till all these
things be fulfilled.*

Every person is eternal in the spirit. For the spirit is timeless.
And, in the depth of his nature, each person is spirit. This is not
understood by most people because they are mired in a material
mind-set with its division of experience into units of incremental
time. These things screen the person's awareness from the
timeless depth of his nature. Thus it is the same to say of a
person, that he *will be* cleansed, as it is to say that he *is* cleansed.
In the first instance, the person's experience is spread out over

90

time. That is how his material mind perceives it. In the second, the before and after of his experience lie together in timeless unity within him. In either case, material-mindedness is removed and spiritual-mindedness is realized in its place. So what precisely is meant by the statement, "This generation shall not pass, till all these things be fulfilled"? It is that the transformation is immediate, though it appears to be experienced over time.

Then shall two be in the field; the one shall be taken, and the other left. Two women shall be grinding at the mill; the one shall be taken, and the other left. Watch therefore: for you know not what hour your Lord does come.

The material mind-set will be removed. And the spiritual mind-set, which was always present but screened from awareness by the material mind-set, will remain. This is a matter of spirit, which can neither be set on a timetable nor located in a place. It must be recognized and understood in the spirit.

But know this, that if the goodman of the house had known in what watch the thief would come, he would have watched, and would not have suffered his house to be broken up. Therefore be you also ready: for in such an hour as you think not the Son of man comes.

Both the individual and general spiritual transformations will come not by outward signs, but by inward signs. So look for this inward change in yourself and in the attitude and demeanor of others. But beware of false appearances. For it is the character of the inner person you seek to recognize.

Who then is a faithful and wise servant, whom his lord has made ruler over his household, to give them meat in due season? Blessed is that servant, whom his lord when he comes shall find so doing. Verily I say to you, That he shall make him ruler over all his goods. But and if that evil servant shall say in his heart, My lord delays his coming; And shall begin to smite his fellow servants, and to eat and drink with the drunken; The lord of that servant shall come in a day when he looks not for him, and in an hour that he is not aware of, And shall cut him asunder, and appoint him his portion with the hypocrites: there shall be weeping and gnashing of teeth.

The faithful spiritual person will govern herself wisely, living according to the spirit. This leads to inner growth. And greater spiritual strength and dominion over the self will come from it. But if the unfaithful person allows herself to fall away from the spirit and to submit her will to material motives, she will, without realizing it, lose sight of the spirit altogether. And great will be her sense of alienation from her true self. Self-contradiction, division from others, and general isolation and sorrow will result from this.

Then shall the kingdom of heaven be likened to ten virgins, which took their lamps, and went forth to meet the bridegroom. And five of them were wise, and five were foolish. They that were foolish took their lamps, and took no oil with them: But the wise took oil in their vessels with their lamps. While the bridegroom tarried, they all slumbered and slept. And at midnight there was a cry made, Behold, the bridegroom comes; go you out to meet him. Then all those virgins arose, and trimmed their lamps. And the foolish said to the wise, Give us of your oil; for our lamps are gone out. But the wise answered, saying, Not so; lest there be not enough for us and you: but go you rather to them that sell, and buy for yourselves. And while they went to buy, the bridegroom came; and they that were ready went in with him to the marriage: and the door was shut. Afterward came also the other virgins, saying, Lord, Lord, open to us. But he answered and said, Verily I say to you, I know you not.

Spirit is consciousness. And, if the more encompassing spiritual character of that consciousness is recognized and nurtured, it will grow in the mind. It is in this way that a state of spiritual-mindedness is developed. But, after the initial embrace of the character of spirit, it must be cultivated, so that it will come to fill every corner of the mind. Thus the lamps of the parable are that consciousness recognized as spirit. The oil is the care which makes the lamps produce light, so that a person may see in a spiritual way. To neglect the cultivation of spirit is to neglect the life of spirit. And to neglect it is not to be ready to enter more fully into it. Not to enter more fully into it is to grow further apart from it.

For the kingdom of heaven is as a man travelling into a far country, who called his own servants, and delivered to them his goods. And to one he gave five talents, to another two, and to another one; to every man according to his several ability; and straightway took his journey. Then he that had received the five talents went and traded with the same, and made them other five talents. And likewise he that had received two, he also gained other two. But he that had received one went and dug in the earth, and hid his lord's money. After a long time the lord of those servants comes, and reckons with them. And so he that had received five talents came and brought other five talents, saying, Lord, you delivered to me five talents: behold, I have gained beside them five talents more. His lord said to him, Well done, you good and faithful servant: you have been faithful over a few things, I will make you ruler over many things: enter you into the joy of your lord. He also that had received two talents came and said, Lord, you delivered to me two talents: behold, I have gained two other talents beside them. His lord said to him, Well done, good and faithful servant; you have been faithful over a few things, I will make you ruler over many things: enter you into the joy of your lord. Then he which had received the one talent came and said, Lord, I knew you that you are a hard man, reaping where you have not sown, and gathering where you have not strewn: And I was afraid, and went and hid your talent in the earth: lo, there you have that is thine. His lord answered and said unto him, You wicked and slothful servant, you knew that I reap where I sowed not, and gather where I have not strewn: You ought therefore to have put my money to the exchangers, and then at my coming I should have received mine own with usury. Take therefore the talent from him, and give it to him which has ten talents. For to every one that has shall be given, and he shall have abundance: but from him that has not shall be taken away even that which he has. And cast you the unprofitable servant into outer darkness: there shall be weeping and gnashing of teeth.

This also concerns a nurturing of the life of the spirit and follows the same pattern of development as the previous parable.

The multiplication of talents is the nurturing of spiritual life. The nurturing produces an increase in spiritual wealth: "You have been faithful over a few things, I will make you ruler over many things." The lack of a multiplication of talents results in a loss of what little spiritual life there had been: "For to every one that has shall be given, and he shall have abundance: but from him that has not shall be taken away even that which he has." This parable also includes the fact that different people have different abilities. Hence the different talents provided at the beginning. The point is that whatever abilities a person has, he should use them to further the growth of the spirit within him. The person who was afraid to do anything with the talent he had was a person who did not truly wish to know or understand the spirit. So he shied away from and neglected it. Those who nurtured the spirit grew stronger in it, until it filled their minds and lives. In this way, they entered fully into the life of the spirit. But the one who shied away from and neglected the spirit was left in the darkness of a materially determined life. Here he languished with all the bitterness and frustration of a life hemmed in by material limitation, where there is no awareness of a hope of deliverance.

When the Son of man shall come in his glory, and all the holy angels with him, then shall he sit upon the throne of his glory: And before him shall be gathered all nations: and he shall separate them one from another, as a shepherd divides his sheep from the goats: And he shall set the sheep on his right hand, but the goats on the left. Then shall the King say to them on his right hand, Come, you blessed of my Father, inherit the kingdom prepared for you from the foundation of the world: For I was hungry, and you gave me meat: I was thirsty, and you gave me drink: I was a stranger, and you took me in: Naked, and you clothed me: I was sick, and you visited me: I was in prison, and you came to me. Then shall the righteous answer him, saying, Lord, when saw we you hungry, and fed you? or thirsty, and gave you drink? When saw we you a stranger, and took you in? or naked, and clothed you? Or when saw we you sick, or in prison, and came to you? And the King shall answer and say to them, Verily I say to you, Inasmuch as you have done it to one of the least of these my brethren, you have done it to me. Then shall he say also to them on the left hand, Depart from me, you cursed, into everlasting fire, prepared for the devil and his angels: For I was hungry, and you gave me no meat: I was thirsty, and you gave me no drink: I was a stranger, and you took me not in: naked, and you clothed me not: sick, and in prison, and you visited me not. Then shall they also answer him, saying, Lord, when saw we you hungry, or athirst, or a stranger, or naked, or sick, or in prison, and did not minister to you? Then shall he answer them, saying, Verily I say to you, Inasmuch as you did it not to one of the least of these, you did it not to me. And these shall go away into everlasting punishment: but the righteous into life eternal.

When the full glory of the spiritual life comes, what remains of divisiveness, anger, etc. will be cleansed from the minds of people. And only the purity of a spiritually-minded life will remain. The good traits listed above are those which arise from the sense of unity in a spiritually-minded life. The bad traits, or traits reflecting a neglect of this sense of unity, are anger, jealousy, spite, vindictiveness, cunning, hate, conflict, thirst for material advantage, all coming from the sense of a general isolation of the person—that is, a lack of the sense of unity. This is what leads people not to minister to the needs of others. For they fear them and want to upstage them in the material competition of life. Where individuals had been left to languish in material limitation, now the traits which made them that way will be left behind in that limited domain. For all will be restored, the spiritual first, the materially-minded last. Both in accordance with whatever good there is in them, even though it be but a small remnant in some of them.

And he took the cup, and gave thanks, and gave it to them, saying, Drink you all of it; For this is my blood of the new testament, which is shed for many for the remission of sins. But I say to you, I will not drink henceforth of this fruit of the vine, until that day when I drink it new with you in my Father's kingdom.

Jesus will give his life for the truth which he has taught. That truth will set humanity free from a materially-minded existence. A materially-minded existence is the cause of sin. Thus the remission of sins is the removal of their cause. After his death, Jesus will enter into the fullness of spiritual being. And it is in this way that he will appear to his disciples.

What, could you not watch with me one hour? Watch and pray, that you enter not into temptation: the spirit indeed is willing, but the flesh is weak.

In the present material condition of humanity, it is very difficult for an individual person to maintain a spiritual perspective. The person easily slips back into material-mindedness, even though he wills to do otherwise. This is because he is surrounded by a very convincing array of material circumstance. Life is difficult and punishes any neglect of material needs. Moreover, most people do not exercise any sort of spiritual perspective. So it does not take much for this to interfere with a spiritual person's state of mind. Consequently, such a person must seek the things of the spirit all the more in order to remain under their influence.

And, behold, one of them which were with Jesus stretched out his hand, and drew his sword, and struck a servant of the high priest's, and smote off his ear. Then said Jesus to him, Put up again your sword into his place: for all they that take the sword shall perish with the sword.

The sword is an instrument of divisiveness. Those who persist in living in that state of mind will become more deeply enmeshed in it and will eventually be lost to it throughout the remainder of their lives.

[Immediately following the above statement] Think you that I cannot now pray to my Father, and he shall presently give me more than twelve legions of angels? But how then shall the scriptures be fulfilled, that thus it must be?

Do not underestimate the mystery of the spirit of God. Even in a spiritual state, people cannot fathom its purposes. So to live in the spirit is to submit to it as well, knowing that its purposes are beyond human understanding, whether the human being in question be in a material or a spiritual state of mind.

98

All power is given to me in heaven and in earth.

All power is given to Jesus in the spirit and in the material. For the material is ultimately the work of the spirit and subordinate to it. Once a person (in this case, Jesus) has entered into the full possession of a spiritual mind, the true character of the material is understood. Its ways and purposes are recognized as being coordinated with the workings of spirit. As a result, there is no anguish, no division or disharmony.

Transcendent Dignity

To shift momentarily to another part of scriptural literature, the Jewish portion, there are insights found here as well which connote an interest relative to what has just been shown. In the book of Genesis, the story of the Garden of Eden conveys a subtle distinction between the nature of spiritual humanity and a strictly material humanity.

This is a dramatization of what has come to be known in Semitic religion as the "fall" of humankind. So the question is, what does this fall suggest? In examining the narrative, one sees that in the beginning there are two freshly minted human beings in a beautiful and peaceful garden watered by gentle springs. They are naked. For they have no shame. What is natural is good. And there is nothing to hide.

As pure intelligences in material form, they know each other's thoughts and emotions. And there are no mutually harmful thoughts or emotions. For they have no fear, which is what begets malice, envy, and hate. They know the heart of God as well as they know each other. But they do not know the mind of spirit. For they are yet limited, individual beings, which means they are limited in the spirit. In other words, they are individual within a unity of spirit which is greater than themselves.

The way in which they know the spirit is as a child knows its parents, which is to say that they are aware of its benevolent disposition toward them. For their minds are unencumbered by a confining material mind-set. So the oneness of spirit flows freely through them. There is a transcendence from one person to another and between each person and universal spirit (or universal consciousness), without this openness violating the individual uniqueness of either one of them.

Each person knows he or she is a fully realized expression of spirit, God, or universal consciousness. But, unlike universal spirit, the consciousness of each of them is limited as to content, making them material beings. Nevertheless, they are spiritualized material beings who thoroughly understand their grounding in spirit. For God takes the form of self-limiting spirit in each of them. And they have not been cut off from this source.

Moreover, the same spirit, in a somewhat less limited character, is also both of them together. For their material experience, emanating from universal spirit, is the fluid which coordinates and links them in one mutual world. This world is themselves and the garden. Thus spirit is a consciousness which is individual, multiply individual, and universal. But, as consciousness in general, it is simply awareness. So it is in this manner that awareness can be confined to a single individual, unite one individual with another in a common milieu of experience, and also separately express its own universal, all-inclusive character.

In any case, what is significant is that spirit is one and the same thing, limited only in the manner of its encompassment. In its individual expressions in the present example, it limits itself to one person, to another person, and to both of them together. Yet it is also all-inclusive in its fundamental character. So, since in their original innocent condition the two denizens of the garden are immersed in both limited and universal awareness, they partake principally of the limited form but also somewhat of the universal as well. This means that, while they are individually limited, they are able to experience their common unity in a greater oneness.

Then comes the "fall." This is representative of today's individual human isolation. It is symbolized as originating from the eating of the fruit of the tree of the knowledge of good and evil. Up to this point, the man and woman have known only the good. So what is evil? They want to know, not understanding that such knowledge will subject them to a condition of divisiveness and mutual opposition, not only between themselves but with everything. They ask themselves and one another: could this knowledge be an expansion beyond the limits of our present awareness? Surely it is something we should know about.

But, taking the fruit, they discover that it leads not to an expansion of understanding and experience, but to greater limitation. For example, they can no longer directly discern one another's thoughts and emotions. Neither do they know God. Universal spirit, it would seem, has slipped away from them. Their minds have become wholly material, limited to material awareness alone.

Not knowing one another, they cover themselves out of shame. What is shame? It is fear of the other's opinion. And this they no longer have any insight into. Though together, they are strangers. From the present moment forward, all their race will be strangers to one another. Thus the story goes, as it unfolds a perfect representation of the material human condition.

Moreover, they have no idea what God is. For they know only the material, since the awareness of each of them is now restricted to the content of his or her individual consciousness. Universal spirit has become a ghost, a chilling wind coming only fitfully to each of them over the barren reaches of the unknown.

So they hide. Hiding and shame, which is another form of hiding, make them unfit for the eternal peace of the garden. There will be conflict. Restless, forever seeking ways of breaking out of the tomblike encasement of their material lives, their suspicion, envy, enmity, and greed declare that they must find other quarters more fitting to their mind-set. So they are forced to leave the garden, as they have already left the spirit.

Now in the material world universal spirit is little understood. So in multitudinous ingenious ways, the idea of God is inevitably clothed with human attributes: greed, jealousy, anger, even in some cases concupiscence. It is, and will be, a long road to get from this state of mind to a spiritual mind-set. For such occluded, materially oriented minds, reacquainting themselves with the spirit is no easy matter. Consequently, humanity must progress through numerous permutations of understanding.

Because of the familiarity of the material and the unfamiliarity of the spirit, there is a powerful tendency for people to clothe every spiritual expression in some form of material representation. The tendency to give God human attributes is the most common such act. But another tendency is for human beings to take sacrifices, images, sacraments, and even written scriptures to be objects of direct spiritual communion. It is as though, by embracing these material representations, the individual person believes he will be granted some portion of spiritual being, some connection with the eternal.

Not so. Take the scriptures, which are in the minds of many the most sacred of these expressions. Scripture is not spirit. No matter how much spiritual insight is contained within a scripture, that insight must be written in and limited to some form of human language. It must be confined to a human understanding, as it is expressed by such an understanding.

It is not universal spirit. It is not even a product of a pure intelligence in material form. Rather, a scripture is a carrier of spiritual insight. It communicates something conceptually ineffable. So there, in the ineffably inexpressible, is its truth and its power. The written language is merely an opaque lens which seeks to transfer the spiritual insight to a human mind. That insight is awkwardly seized upon by a finite mind as it is transferred to it by means of the written text. It is in this form that the insight is presented to a human understanding. The truth of it is what is of interest, not the unreliable means of its communication.

It is not the writing that matters, but the heartfelt recognition of those fragments of truth which are contained within it. Only this truth is worthy of reverence. And it is a truth which is always partial and ongoing in development. Whereas, in the written scripture itself, the perfume of spirit is inextricably mixed with an unclean odor of materially-bound thought and sensibility.

So a movement toward spirit can only be achieved within spirit. For there is always an open window, though the shades appear to be drawn. Universal spirit exists within the heart of humanity. It has never departed from that place. It must so exist, since human beings are in the deepest sense spiritual beings. They are sons of God.

But they are not realized sons. They are not yet sons of God in man, or sons of man, like Jesus. They are not so because they are not filled with a reverence for all things spiritual. Rather, the presence of a spiritual awareness within them is faint and generally ignored. It is entangled and smothered by an exaggerated importance of material concerns. Nevertheless, it is there, simply because consciousness is there. And consciousness is spirit.

So none of what has been commented upon concerning the Gospel of Matthew and referred to as a general spiritual transformation will work as long as most people are unwilling to reform themselves into the creatures of spirit they truly are. For a general transformation cannot be fully achieved on an isolated individual basis.

That has never been successful, as is exemplified by the various religious traditions and their minimal effect on human character. Nevertheless, those who have made the transition are to be respected and commended for their good will and for their efforts in advancing spiritual understanding.

A small number have progressed considerably, reaching the very gates of universal change both in terms of themselves and as a pathway for others. And a very few, like Jesus and the Buddha, have fully crossed over into spirit and shown the way. But, even then, in regard to what other people have been able to understand of their teachings, there are limited and conflicting views.

For these spiritual guides were not completely independent beacons in a wide ocean of generalized awareness. Though transcendent in their powerful insights, they reflected their particular cultures, using the language and concepts familiar to them and to those of similar background to whom they addressed themselves.

It is the limited character of the concepts being used, concepts which were originally employed for other purposes, that has done so much to retard spiritual progress. And it is this same cultural isolation which has also created enemies in truth. Thus there have been blocks of sincerely striving spiritual human beings warring against other blocks of sincerely striving spiritual human beings.

So nothing less that a worldwide spiritual revolution is needed. Men and women of all races, ethnicities, and nationalities must come to recognize the importance of this transformation and join together in bringing it about. Universal selfishness, unregulated physical appetites leading to sensory enslavement, and oppositional material, or partially material, mind-states in general cannot be eradicated in any other way.

In its present condition, the human race is dominated by ego. Even when it purports to be spiritual it is largely so. This works in the following manner. Human beings are creatures of spirit, the vast majority of whom do not know that they are. In fact, it is generally the case that, due to fears generated by material limitations in perspective, they do not wish to know that they are.

They have become so accustomed to these limitations of material life that they cannot imagine any other condition. Consequently they fear both the transformation in outlook and one another. And they hide, each in his singular isolation, under a shell of physical and psychological defensive measures.

Neither do they want to so much as try to envision passing over mentally into a spiritual life, if it involves such a serious, and what they see as difficult, transformation. They would rather do without any guarantor of inner or outer peace and rely on institutions which discipline behavior by force and only incidentally supply any sort of spiritual support by means of religious placebos.

A religious placebo is something which is assumed to represent spiritual life, but which is itself material in character. That covers most of what is done, reverenced, and said in institutional religious practice. This is why Jesus worked outside of the established temple religion of his time. Its ideals were right, but not its practice.

Nonetheless, there is a possible alternative condition of the human race, however unnoticeable or unapproachable it may appear to most people. Its importance lies in the fact that it is the true ground of human existence. It is humanity's home, to which it has always been a rightful heir. As the unlimited, indivisible character of pure consciousness demonstrates—when it is observed without reference to its content—human beings are spiritual in their core nature, regardless of the beguiling and threatening mental impressions which hourly and daily bedazzle their senses.

In very early childhood this spiritual core in human personality is, in fact, recognized and known by the child. But, as the English poet William Wordsworth expressed the problem in his "Ode on Intimations of Immortality," the close connection with spirit is soon lost. It is overwhelmed and flooded out by material concerns.

This is because the "pure consciousness" just mentioned is exclusively filled with, and limited to, a finite content which the human mind, in its practical interest, gradually constructs into a closely interwoven material fabric. This web-like barrier of the mind, with its quick but not so subtle imaginings and its complex reasonings, is what a person comes to recognize as the material world.

He even begins to believe he too is limited in the same way as the sensory stuff of his mind. For to him human consciousness increasingly takes on the appearance of an inexplicable and fragile bubble floating in a mass of limited and limiting minutia. He knows that, when considered in a piecemeal fashion, none of this minutia is really important. So he believes he must assume that neither is his seemingly expendable individual consciousness important. It will be discarded after an average span of seventy-some years or so.

But, at the same time, he cannot forget that the center of both his individual being and his world, which center is his pure consciousness, is not limited like everything which it is aware of. That is, it is not limited like everything other than itself. This opposition between the experience of pure consciousness and the experience of the material sets up a conflict within him.

It is what the apostle Paul referred to in the epistle to the Romans as a warfare in his members. It arises from a desire to be that consciousness, to cling to it, to be utterly free of limitation, as pure consciousness is perceived to be. But, alas, nothing else in experience supports that desire. There is limitation everywhere. So the person sighs and surrenders to the material, more or less.

"More or less" because he cannot let go of this feeling of a potentially unfettered freedom, which he recognizes without any material evidence to support it. So he acts within the material sphere out of a desire for that liberty without wholly believing in it. He develops what is commonly understood to be an ego. This ego expresses a sense of the importance of self without any conviction of it.

All around him the world is frustratingly limiting in its character. It is full of pain, disappointment, suffering, death, and decay. It has everywhere in it the creeping stench of the grave. Nowhere is there seen to be any relief, no way to get out of this little box of material existence, full of spinning razors and turning gears designed to sever and grind flesh into a senseless and unthinking pulp. Even stars and planets have a limited existence. Yet the will of the man or woman presses on as best it can.

Each person enters into battle with his world. He says, "I will not be pushed aside. I will not be limited. I will not perish any sooner than necessary. Neither will I succumb to a position of personal insignificance or undeserved shame. I will triumph, if only for a little while. I will only go down to oblivion when I must, hammering with my fists on the inner lid of my coffin and shouting where no one can hear."

But the world pushes back. And the warrior becomes weary. Enter religion in its usual form. Its spiritual founder has often meant to communicate something more, be he Moses, the Buddha, Jesus, or Muhammad. But in the end the religion becomes, or is reduced to, a promise of better things in the next life and little more. The warrior takes hold of this inferior weapon and limps onward, wounded and low-spirited, sometimes angry and wishing to crush any contrary opinion, though the one he has is feeble enough.

Herein lies the attitude of mean-spiritedness. It says, "I will hope for the best, whatever that might be. Meanwhile, I will get what I can out of this life. I will shove, push, and take what ought to be rightfully mine, maybe even a little, or quite a bit, more." Either such a person, which is nearly everyone in some degree, will think: I do not care what others think. Or he will decide: I will conceal my designs. In most cases it is the latter. Thus the prevalence of hypocrisy and deceit in the world. Thus the universal phenomenon of the betrayal of humankind by humankind.

This is what Jesus of Nazareth saw. What he tried to ameliorate. But his disciples did not fully understand him. They thought he was advocating some kind of emotional love, applying it like oil to a gearbox to make things mesh in a smoother way. But simple respect for spiritual being, both in and out of humankind, they did not understand. And the world has followed in their train. Today the human race is not much better than it ever was. More subtle perhaps. And possessed of greater cunning: it hides some of its cruelties while being unable to conceal others.

Yet the teachings of Jesus were not in vain. A thing of such great beauty cannot be hidden from the heart and mind forever. It will shine out, like the sun coming from behind parting clouds. But, for this to happen on a world-changing scale, deceit must be removed. The cunning of men must be set aside. And all hierarchies established by the presumptuous few to dominate the many should be ignored. For these hierarchies are the setting up of some people over others with a greater authority than is plainly natural. And ultimately it is for the benefit of the few.

When these changes have been made, two things will remain. First, the heart of God will burst forth within the heart of man. For the two are the same. Spirit is the inner person in self-limiting form. Second, each person will know himself in his transcendent dignity. And everyone will recognize his brother and sister as being the same as he is in spiritual station, though individually and, yes, materially unique. Then, with an unprecedented forcefulness, trust, honor, and decency will become commonplace.

Made in the USA
Middletown, DE
06 December 2020

26417382R00066